Sir Gawain and the Green Knight

MANCHESTER
UNIVERSITY PRESS

Sir Gawain and the Green Knight

revised edition

*edited, with an introduction,
prose translation and notes,
by W. R. J. Barron*

Manchester University Press

First edition published 1974 by Manchester University Press
Reprinted in paperback 1976, 1979, 1984, 1988, 1991, 1994, 1998

This edition published 2001 by
Manchester University Press
Oxford Road, Manchester M13 9NR, UK
www.manchesteruniversitypress.co.uk

British Library Cataloguing-in-Publication Data
A catalogue record for this book is available from the British Library

ISBN 0 7190 5517 2 *paperback*

This edition first published 1998

08 07 06 05 04 03 02 01 10 9 8 7 6 5 4 3 2

Typeset in Bembo
by Koinonia, Manchester
Printed in Great Britain
by Clays Ltd, St Ives plc

Contents

To the memory of my mother
Elizabeth Jane McMinn

Preface

The Preface to the first edition of this book, published in 1974, has a somewhat apologetic tone, as if the presentation of a classic medieval text with a literal translation in parallel were a rather dubious academic exercise. And indeed several reviewers, while in general approving its execution, wondered whether such a project, savouring so much of the classroom crib, should ever have been undertaken. Twenty-four years later there seems no need to be so defensive.

The use of medieval literature primarily as a battlefield for philologists has given way to appreciation of it for its own sake. Much of that change is due to *Sir Gawain and the Green Knight*. The vividness of the images it evokes, the liveliness of its fusion of courtly and colloquial diction, the zest of a narrative which encourages conventional expectations only to undermine them constantly, the multi-layered meaning of a moral detective-story inviting the reader to cooperate in the creative process, have won it a wider audience year by year.

And not just in the ever-expanding British universities. Students in sixth form colleges, introduced to this contemporary of Chaucer, appreciate in the *Gawain*-poet the same oblique wisdom without didacticism, the same humanity making medieval convention meaningful for their own lives. Continental readers recognise the thematic subtlety of Chrétien de Troyes already touched with the affectionate irony of Cervantes. New World audiences find his old world values, his idealism tempered with realism, fully accessible. Translations abound in many languages; a classic of English literature is finding its audience in the wider world.

Proof of its classic status is its power to inspire other works of art: films, TV adaptations, music, theatre, opera, dance. Not yet, but someday soon perhaps, the classic film which its spare, concrete narrative, vivid images, and filmic framing of action anticipate.

The wider audience justifies a wider variety of editions. Among the many which exist, this version aims to provide a conservative text with the minimum of editorial intrusion, presented in parallel with a close, literal translation. As in any prose version of a poem, much is lost; still more here, no doubt, in the attempt to reveal the original by removing the obscuring varnish of a language grown dim with age. How much of its surface brilliance is damaged, how far its texture and colour values are altered in the process, can at least be judged by comparison with the original text.

My thanks are due to the friends who gave generously of their scholarship and good taste to modify the potential damage: John Anderson, Ida Gordon, Elspeth Kennedy. I must also express my indebtedness to the trustees of the British Library, to the council of the Early English Text Society, and to Oxford University Press for permission to print the text from the facsimile of B. L. MS Cotton Nero A.x, ART. 3.

Introduction

Sir Gawain and the Green Knight is a romance. The form, like the word, is French in origin, evidence of the dominant influence of France on the culture of medieval England. That influence was at its peak when, about the middle of the twelfth century, French tastes in narrative literature underwent a marked change. Until then the feudal nobility who were patrons of literature had preferred the national epic—stories of Charlemagne and his vassals, sometimes united in defence of France and the Christian faith against the Moors of Spain, at others opposed in a struggle between royal tyranny on one side and independence of spirit on the other. In either case the action was predominantly military, battle and siege interrupted only by council of war and victory feast. The values expressed were those of a warrior society, communally and unquestioningly held but personified in individuals of pre-eminent heroic stature. Heroines were unknown in this man's world, where the only women were shadowy background figures: noble mothers, chaste wives or patiently waiting betrothed. The change, when it came, affected first the role of women—not in the national epic, which continued to flourish side by side with the new form, but in contemporary versions of the legends of Greece and Rome. The classical epic had acknowledged the importance—however transitory—in the hero's life of the women he loved, as Achilles did Polyxena, or who had the misfortune to love him, as Dido and Lavinia loved Aeneas. French versions, probably made between 1150 and 1160, greatly elaborated this element, in scope and also in significance, treating emotion not merely as the motive for heroic action but as something of inherent interest, to be analysed for its own sake. The romantic principle had been reborn in medieval literature.

The romance proper evolved during the following decades in the work of a writer of genius exploring fresh subject-matter. The Matter of Britain—legends of King Arthur and his wonder-working companions, heroes of forgotten epics and gods of dead religions—was already some six centuries old. Having long survived, in oral form and heavily intermixed with myth and fairy-tale, amongst the Celtic peoples of Ireland, Wales, Cornwall and Brittany, it achieved literary respectability in the Latin pseudo-chronicle of Geoffrey of Monmouth (1138) and popularity amongst educated laymen in French adaptations of Geoffrey's work. It provided narrative poets with an 'historical' setting—the empire of Arthur, victor over the Saxon invaders, conqueror of Western Europe, defiant rival of the Roman emperor—with an identifiable world free from the epic associations and factual restraints of story-matter previously exploited, but a world in which the element of fairy-tale made all things possible. The genius of Chrétien de Troyes transformed it into a mirror for his own world, reflecting the manners, architecture and dress of aristocratic society and the values of its members, refined and heightened by romantic idealism. The basis of society was still military, but the heroic ideal had been transmuted into the chivalric code which governed behaviour off the battlefield as minutely as on it. War had, indeed, largely given way to joust and duel, communal action to rivalry for pre-eminence, service of faith and nation to fidelity to the code. And in that code devotion to women was a primary article: protection of the weak was the professional concern of knights errant, only the brave deserved the fair, and the love of a noble woman inspired the perfect practice of chivalry—most perfectly when she was unattainable, already married to another.

Chrétien was not the only French poet, nor even the first, to see Arthurian matter as the perfect medium for the expression of contemporary ideals. His unique contribution lay in the development of a narrative technique by which events are so ordered, commented upon, explained or deliberately left unexplained as to compose a thematic scheme. Superficially the narrative may appear incoherent, overcrowded with incident, full of improbable coincidences and loose ends, yet Chrétien was a skilful story-teller, holding the interest of his audience while he directed their attention to problems inherent in contemporary ideals: the conflicting claims of marriage and knight errantry, of romantic love and social duty, of obedience to the whims of a mistress or to the dictates of honour. No definitive answers were given, but the questioning process brought more subtle understanding of the code.

The code itself posed problems, not least the ranking of its component elements, each considered as an absolute. Those who followed Chrétien in the late twelfth and early thirteenth centuries established supreme heroes, each representing chivalric perfection, each in turn supplanted by another: Gawain, the exemplar of physical prowess and courteous behaviour, was outranked by Lancelot, whose knighthood was inspired by love of Guinevere, Arthur's wife, and he in turn was surpassed by his son Galahad, for whom the supreme achievement of chivalry was the service of religion in the quest for the Holy Grail. The loose narrative structure of the romance allowed the adventures of several knights to be interlinked, the lesser serving as foils for the supreme hero. As verse gave way to prose, larger and more elaborate structures became possible, cyclic romances covering the whole scope of Arthurian 'history', weaving together episodes originally independent and interconnecting hitherto unrelated themes. The more complex and crowded the canvas became, the greater the fascination it exercised upon the medieval imagination, embodying a world in which the highest aspirations of contemporary society were realised. The romance was to evolve still further in structure and content during the fourteenth and fifteenth centuries, but it was in the work of Chrétien and his immediate successors that the Matter of Britain made its greatest impact on Western Europe, being translated, adapted and imitated in all the major languages.

England, however, lagged behind. The legends of Arthur held particular significance for the English, who thought of him as their fellow countryman, one-time conqueror of the lands in France to which they still laid claim, the 'hope of the British' who would return to help them in their hour of need. But the Norman conquest, which had made the English aristocracy French-speaking, given them estates in France and involved them in constant wars to retain them, also made them free of the whole store of romance in the original language. English versions came late, mostly in the fourteenth and fifteenth centuries, often clumsily abbreviated and showing more interest in narrative than in ideas. The audience for such adaptations was, perhaps, not the most refined: those of the minor nobility no longer wholly at ease in French and members of the rising middle class. The texts which have survived may not be representative, but in general they compare unfavourably with the best French examples.

The comparison would be even less favourable but for the survival of a single, shabby little manuscript now in the British Library. Ms Cotton Nero A.x, art. 3, copied in a hand of about 1400, contains four poems in the dialect of the north-west midlands, written during the latter part of the fourteenth century and all apparently by the same author. We do not know who he was, but from his own work we can see that he was widely read in the most sophisticated literature of the age, religious and secular, English, French and Latin. He was a provincial, writing in the dialect of his region and in the alliterative verse traditional there, but on the evidence of his poetry he had an intimate knowledge of aristocratic life, architecture, etiquette, hunting, feasting, dress and armour, and the terms of courtly conversation. He may well have lived in one of the great castles of Lancashire, Staffordshire or Derbyshire where John of Gaunt kept court, as secretary or chaplain. One thing, however, is certain: he was a writer of genius. Of his four poems, two, the biblical homilies *Purity* and *Patience*, rank high in Middle English literature, and two amongst the masterpieces of any period. One is *Sir Gawain*, the other is the religious poem *Pearl*, an elegy expressed as a dream allegory, in which the conventional debate form is used to clarify a theological issue. The components are familiar, yet the poem is unique; not merely because the poet is master of all the conventions and the theme—the right of the innocent to salvation—is a vital one, but because the whole is vitalised and fused together by the power of feeling, by the poet's grief for his daughter who died in infancy.

I

In *Sir Gawain*, too, the conventions have been revitalised by the intensity of the poet's involvement with his subject-matter. When it was written the romance was already a dying form, sinking under the weight of traditional ideals, traditional subjects, traditional methods of presentation. The *Gawain* poet was soaked in romance tradition, and how thoroughly he understood it his poem shows at every point. It begins, as a romance should, at a high festival in Arthur's court, one of the periodic renewals of Round Table unity, idealism and loyalty to the king. It is an occasion for conventional usages, the familiar rituals of jousting and dancing in a world of unstinted luxury and carefree merry-making (37–47), a world described in superlatives, distanced from and unrivalled by the readers' own society, which, nevertheless, it closely resembles (48–59). Everything in the celebration of Christmas and New Year—chapel service, gift-giving and games, the hierarchical assembly at table in order of reputation (60–73, 109–15), the ceremonious service of the meal to bursts of music (116–29)—is ordered, formal, customary. Only Arthur's absence from the table seems out of keeping; but this is itself a convention of romance, accepted without explanation as the king's accustomed usage (85–106). His expectation of adventure evokes the conventional response (132–222): the visitant who appears, his challenge and the response to it conform to familiar patterns of romance. The challenge is to the society as a whole (223–315), but traditionally it is the king who responds, stung by imputations against the reputation of the Round Table (316–38). By convention Arthur is the initiator and stimulator of chivalric adventure, the arbiter in affairs of honour and the rewarder of knightly achievement, only very rarely himself an actor: individual knights act as representatives of king, court and knighthood itself. With the courteous intervention of Gawain, claiming the adventure as his own by traditional right as the first to ask it (339–74), the real hero of the romance emerges. He is faced with an improbable compact of a kind common enough in romance, to exchange blows with his opponent, neither defending himself (375–416). It seems to imply certain death for the challenger; that he survives so improbably (417–39) would surprise no reader of romance, familiar with the giants, wizards and enchantresses who figure there and the frequent interference of the supernatural in human affairs. But his survival places Gawain in a dilemma: by the terms of the compact he must present himself at the Green Chapel on next New Year's Day to receive a similar blow or, as the challenger reminds him, be accounted a coward (440–56). It is a familiar dilemma in romance, where characteristically the hero must choose between apparently certain death on one hand and some shameful breach of the chivalric code on the other. For a true knight both cowardice and compromise are equally unthinkable; but he has only to grapple boldly with one alternative or the other and the dilemma will disappear, leaving chivalric values confirmed and his personal reputation enhanced. The romance is, after all, an idealistic medium.

In *Sir Gawain* too the dilemma is grasped; the compact is kept and yet death is avoided. But the superficial conformity of plot is deceptive: its successful resolution leaves the hero writhing in shame, accusing himself of cowardice and other breaches of the knightly code, in betrayal of his true nature (2369–86). The break with convention is startling, unique: other romances may show knights in defeat the better to heighten the success of some more perfect chivalric personality, and the supreme hero himself may know temporary humiliation, but ultimate failure is unthinkable, still less any implication that the chivalric code is an inadequate guide to human conduct. Departure from the norm is all the more unexpected in *Sir Gawain*, where the conventions of the form are as meticulously observed as in any French romance. Yet in retrospect it is not unprepared for: the careful, almost self-conscious observance of convention is accompanied by innovations which, from the very beginning of the romance, establish an undertone of ambiguity. The opening, locating the events historically and geographically, is itself conventional, drawing on the parallel tradition of Arthurian chronicle which traces the descent of Western chivalry from that of Troy, whose heroes founded the civilisations of Europe (1–24). But the nature of Britain's inheritance is ambiguous: founded *wyth wynne* (joy) by *Felix* (fortunate) *Brutus*, it has ever since been a place of *blysse and blunder*, where bold men made mischief, its reputation associated with that of an archetypal ancestor who was regarded as both famous and notorious.[1] It is left to the reader to draw the implications and relate them to the story that follows. No overt connection is asserted: a deliberate ambiguity of syntax prevents positive identification of the ancestor figure, no judgement can be  made on his *tresoun*, and the undertone of ambiguity produced by the mingling of terms of praise and disparagement might well escape the less perceptive reader, lulled into suspension of judgement by the familiar conventions of a romance proem.

What the proem has to say of the story it introduces is equally ambiguous (25–36): it is a 'real adventure' (*aunter in erde*), yet so extraordinary that some people consider it a marvel, one of *Arthurez wonderez* yet long known in written form. Arthur himself is introduced in terms appropriate to his traditional role as leader of a noble company all *in her first age* (53–9, 85–106): handsome, youthful and gay, noble-minded and eager for chivalric adventure. But some of the terms have overtones which hint at an excess of imperious temper (*hyȝest mon of wylle*), youthful vigour (*ȝep*) carried to the point of childishness  (*childgered*), a restless longing for novelty, and a concern with punctilio (*nobelay*) for its own sake. These qualities are all admirable in themselves, and a king should excel in everything; but excess may be dangerous in the responsible leader of a society where everything is *rych reuel oryȝt and rechles* (carefree/careless) *merþes*.

The visitant whose crashing arrival mingles with the music of the feast (132–6) effectively silences the carefree revelry of the court (232–49). Yet his coming merely fulfils Arthur's expectations, and his role as challenger of the Round Table is formulaic. The court's stunned reaction is perhaps due to an ambiguous mixture of traits in the person of the Green Knight (136–220). Some are normal and acceptable, suggesting a courtly figure from their own world, tall, handsome, robust yet well shaped, dressed in the height of contemporary fashion, with

1 See the note on lines 1–19 below.

rich furs and jewelled embroidery; others utterly out of keeping with such a figure—the monstrous axe, the unfashionable length of hair and beard, above all the incredible greenness of both man and horse—yet familiar as characteristics of the Wild Man of the Wood who figures in some romances as a churlish opponent of chivalry. The elements are familiar, but their fusion in one person is unacceptable, incomprehensible. And the poet is deliberately unhelpful, juxtaposing the  ominous axe and the sprig of holly, a sign of peaceful intent, without comment and avoiding the implications of the Green Knight's giant stature: 'I believe he actually may have been half giant, but at any rate I declare he was the biggest of men'. No wonder the court is silent: what are they—and the audience—to expect of a character quite outside their familiar experience, neither knight nor supernatural creature but a fusion of both?

His behaviour is as ambivalent as his person. His manner towards Arthur and the court is partly polite and deferential (224–31, 256–74), partly arrogant and contemptuous (279–316). And the challenge he issues is as ambiguous as his manner: he chooses to treat it as a game fit for *berdles chylder*, but it implies death either for him or for his opponent. The court's response is itself ambiguous: though their instinctive reaction is to be wary of him, the knights sit passively, unobjecting, while the king takes up the gauntlet. Arthur's reaction as, shamed and angered by the Green Knight's mocking laughter, he darts towards him and seizes his axe to strike the first blow (316–38), is in keeping with the imperious temperament he often displays in romance. Open criticism of the king is unthinkable, and the poet subtly implies that the silence of the court is due to deference towards him as much as to fear of the Green Knight (244–9). Yet Arthur scarcely cuts an impressive figure as he stands making great sweeps with the axe, the Green Knight towering over him, quite unmoved by his extravagant feints; there is something ominous in the reversal of normal expectations, in a passivity which appears more potent than armed force. The outcome of their encounter seems doubtful, threatening the safety of the king, the survival of all the Round Table stands for.

Gawain's intervention is phrased with all the courtesy of a true knight, yet there is implied criticism of the king for taking up so foolish a challenge, and of the court for allowing him to become involved in an adventure which threatens his destruction. His own life, Gawain modestly suggests, would be least loss to the society, and his fellow courtiers hastily agree that the king should be exempted. Arthur persists in treating it as a game and jestingly dismisses the thought of death from the return blow as he surrenders the axe to Gawain (366–74), but serious undertones begin to creep into the affair, a challenge to the security and reputation of the Round Table and doubts as to its motivation in chivalric adventure. They deepen as Gawain and the Green Knight face each other, repeating the terms of the compact with legal exactitude (375–416); an exactitude contrasted with the challenger's refusal to reveal his name and the trysting place for the return match before receiving the blow, the dismissive tone in which he speaks of the blow itself (*buffet, dint, tape*), and his ready acceptance of a personal declaration from Gawain as more appropriate to the festive season than a formal oath. By contrast with his relaxed, ironic manner, Gawain's questions appear tense, but knightly reticence will not allow him to press them to their logical conclusion: is this Christmas game or death-trap?

The striking of the blow provides an answer which is no answer. Its physical effects are described with unblinking, detailed realism; but so also are the supernatural consequences as the Green Knight, holding his severed head in his hand, calmly instructs Gawain to present himself at the Green Chapel for the return blow in a year's time and rides off as mysteriously as he had come (417–61). 'To what land he went none there knew, any more than they knew where he had come from.' The implications are obvious: Gawain must go to what seems certain death or declare himself a coward knight, false to his pledged word. Superficially they are ignored, as the court returns to its feasting (462–90). But under the merry-making ambiguities are rife: all are convinced that they have seen a marvel (*mervayl, selly, wonder*—terms uncommitted to either natural or supernatural) but they make no comment on its significance, and the king, though at heart amazed, dismisses the affair as a Christmas pastime and tells Gawain to hang up his axe as though the matter were closed. Gawain himself is silent. What may—or should—perhaps be in his mind is voiced by the poet himself in one of his rare personal interjections into the third-person narrative: 'Now take good heed, Sir Gawain, that you do not shrink because of danger from pursuing this adventure which you have undertaken.'

II

The first of four movements in the narrative, corresponding to divisions clearly indicated in the manuscript, is over. The break comes at a conventional point, once the dilemma facing the hero has been established. But that dilemma is not to be resolved until the final section; meanwhile other adventures, apparently unconnected, intervene. Narrative tension is maintained, partly by occasional reminders of the fate which hangs over the hero, partly by the same ominous undertone of ambiguity which runs through the first section of the poem. The second opens with a complex passage underlining the ambivalence of the first (491–9)[2]—implying that Arthur's boyish yearning for adventures invoked the apparition of the Green Knight, that his Christmas 'game', proposed in the midst of drinking and merry-making, may be an ill omen for the future, and that the once idle court is now occupied with serious business whose outcome may be unhappy. Throughout the passage the nouns and pronouns are so interchanged as to suggest that not only are Arthur, Gawain and the court equally involved in this ambiguous adventure but that it relates to the common experience of mankind: 'for though men may be light-hearted when they have drunk strong drink, a year passes very quickly, and never brings back like circumstances, the beginning is very seldom like the end'.

The remorselessness of time is then demonstrated in the passing of the year (500–35), a conventional transition justified by the nature of the plot and constructed on a familiar rhetorical pattern, but also a vividly detailed description of growth and decay in Nature: 'all that sprang up in the beginning ripens and decays'. But there is an implied irony: natural time is circular, death is followed by rebirth, while the life of man is linear and his end very different from his beginning. The year of the compact will pass inexorably, but where will Gawain be at its end?

As that end approaches we find him, superficially, just as we left him, at an All Saints' Day feast amongst *much reuel and ryche of þe Rounde Table* (536–65). But the merry-making of the court is no longer *rechles*; though its members gather round the king *to counseyl þe knyȝt*, there is no indication of what hopeful advice they can give *with care at her hert*, secretly regretting 'that one so distinguished as Gawain should have to go on that mission, to suffer a grievous blow, and strike none in return with his sword'—and their thoughts are so ambiguously expressed that the last phrase might be translated 'and never strike another with his sword'. Gawain's behaviour is equally ambiguous: outwardly the same punctiliously polite, formal figure as in the first section of the poem, he

2 See the note on these lines below.

seems, nevertheless, excessively tight-lipped in his allusions to his mission when he asks Arthur's permission to leave: '"You know the nature of this affair, and I do not care to speak to you further about the difficulties involved; it would only be a waste of breath."' There is, perhaps, a note of despair here, disguised as knightly self-control. '"What can one do but plumb to the depths what Fate holds in store, painful and pleasant alike?"' But contemporary readers, unaccustomed to introspection in the romance, might hear only the note of resolve.

Any doubts they might have would be removed by the purely conventional nature of what follows, the ceremonial arming (566–618), a familiar ritual of romance, establishing the character of the hero, not as an individual but as a representative of chivalry whose moral values are symbolically represented by different pieces of the equipment, as his personal eminence is by the richness with which his armour is ornamented. There is much gold on Gawain's armour and gold is the colour of the heraldic device on his shield, the pentangle which symbolises the personal ideal to which he aspires; in knightly achievement and in moral aspiration Gawain himself is 'like refined gold, free from every imperfection, graced with chivalric virtues'. The description, physical and symbolic, of the pentangle is complex (619–65).[3] The five-sided, five-pointed design, attributed to Solomon, the exemplar of wisdom, is presented as a 'perfect' figure, balanced and integrated, each line interlocking with others without overlapping them, unbroken and equally meaningful in any position, reversed or

otherwise. The perfection of the figure, on which the poet insists emphatically, consists in the balanced coherence of its parts; it is surely an emblem of moral perfection in which individual virtues are

subordinated to the whole, each being equally vital and all being vitiated if any one is imperfectly achieved. The individual virtues for which Gawain is renowned are itemised in relation to the fivefold structure of the pentangle: he is faultless in his five senses, never misusing them sinfully; equally so in his five fingers, symbolising the work of his hands; he trusts in the five wounds of Christ, the redeemer; he draws his strength from the five joys of Mary, the intercessor; and he practises five chivalric virtues—*fraunchyse* (generosity, magnanimity), *felaȝschyp* (loyalty to and love of others), *clannes* (freedom from lust), *cortaysye* (courtesy towards and consideration for others) and *pité* (Christian compassion and devotion to duty). The essential unity of these five pentads is expressed in the overall symbolism of the pent-

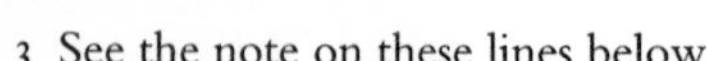

3 See the note on these lines below.

angle, a token of *trawþe*: 'fidelity to others, to promises, to principles; faith in God; moral righteousness; personal integrity'. The word is a summation of Christian chivalry and the symbol identifies Gawain as a perfect exponent of the ideals of the Round Table. Yet the optimistic idealism of the whole passage begs vital questions. Of what use will such splendid equipment be to a knight who must face a brutal blow without defence? And will the integrity which leads him to keep the compact with the Green Knight sustain him under that terrible axe? Chivalric idealism cannot entertain any doubts, and romance does not ask such questions openly.

But what is in Gawain's mind as he rides out in splendour?: 'there and then he took his lance and bade them all good day—for ever, as he thought'. He leaves behind him a deeply troubled court (666–90), convinced that he is going to his death, critical of the king for exposing him to being '"beheaded by an elvish man because of overweening pride"', and anxious to disclaim responsibility for Arthur's decision: '"Who ever knew any king to take such counsel as knights give in quibbling over Christmas games!"' Their outspoken comments provide an ironic contrast with their stunned silence at the first appearance of the Green Knight, their uncertainty as to his nature, and the readiness with which they advised *To ryd þe kyng wyth croun, / And gif Gawan þe game*. And the poet gently underlines the inconsistency of their present grief by the excessive terms and the too insistent alliteration in which he describes it: *Wel much watʒ þe warme water þat waltered of yʒen.*

Meanwhile their chosen representative rides away from the court in Christian confidence but in a more realistic frame of mind: 'Sir Gawain rides in God's name, though no mere game it seemed to him.' On his journey he crosses and re-crosses the borders of romance and reality (691–762).[4] The geography of the romantic imagination, to which the Arthurian kingdom of Logres belongs, gives way to that of north Wales and the Wirral, realistically and exactly described, and that in turn to *contrayeʒ straunge* where Gawain encounters all the perils which lie in wait for knights errant along the paths of romance:

Sumwhyle wyth wormeʒ he werreʒ, and with wolues als,
Sumwhyle wyth wodwos þat woned in þe knarreʒ,
Boþe wyth bulleʒ and bereʒ, and boreʒ oþerquyle,
And etayneʒ þat hym anelede of þe heʒe felle; (720–3)

4 See the note on lines 691–702 below.

But they appear and disappear so rapidly, in such a breathless catalogue of the zoological and the supernatural, that it is difficult to take them seriously. Perhaps we were not intended to: there is a comic excess of alliteration which might seem merely unfortunate if the medium were not so skilfully handled elsewhere. The real threat comes from a different quarter: 'fighting did not so greatly trouble him, the winter weather was worse'. In the characteristic romance, climate, like landscape, scarcely impinges on the consciousness of either reader or protagonist; the knights are affected only by what challenges the code they serve and to them the threat of the elements is irrelevant. For Gawain the challenge of a northern winter, with its freezing sleet and cascading mountain streams, is too keen to ignore, and it is borne in upon the reader by the insistent bite and crash of the alliteration. The knight takes refuge in religion, punctiliously observing, as he does throughout, the duties of his faith. And we find ourselves more and more aware of the individual beneath the armour, the man rather than the knight, unfed and unsheltered, chilled and isolated, with 'no company save his horse among the woods and hills, and no one but God to speak with by the way', our common humanity making us empathise with him.

While he prays for shelter and crosses himself, as if in answer to his prayer a refuge appears (763–806). At first no more than a phantasm 'as it shimmered and shone through the lovely oaks', it grows more and more clearly defined and detailed as Gawain approaches: a castle of the late fourteenth century, still surrounded by heavy defensive walls, turreted and battlemented, but made for luxurious living, with its high-roofed hall crowned with chimneys and carved pinnacles. Can this be an English stronghold beyond the wilderness of Wirral, or one of those chalk-white chateaux of France which decorate the Duc de Berry's *Très Riches Heures*, sharply detailed yet as insubstantial in silhouette as the paper castles decorating the dishes at a feast of which Gawain is reminded by it? Its ambivalent presentation is part of the ambiguity which has persisted ever since Gawain left Camelot: the mingling of the geography of romance with that familiar to the regional audience of the poem, of the conventional trials of knight errantry with the harsh realities of a northern winter, of the vision of a fairy-tale castle chanced upon in the woods with technical details of contemporary architecture, leaves the reader in doubt as to the nature of the experience with which he is being presented. Both elements, literary convention and identifiable experience, are perfectly familiar, nor are they crudely juxtaposed as conflicting aspects of reality; but the subtle alternation of the romantic and the realistic vision, and the undertone of irony associated with the former, are perhaps intended to make the reader more sharply aware of romance conventions and the extent to which they are at variance with his own experience of the world. If he is aware of any discrepancy, he may also be conscious of the hints which have persisted since the beginning of the second section of discrepancies between two aspects of Gawain's nature theoretically indissoluble: the knight, confident in Christian faith and chivalric code, resolutely bent upon the fulfilment of his duty, and the man, isolated, lonely, tormented by hunger and cold, troubled by fear of what lies ahead of him.

Even the immediate prospect is doubtful. The mysterious castle seems innocent enough, but romance tradition allows for various receptions behind the same façade: there are castles where knights errant are honourably entertained in a society like their own, sharing their chivalric values; others where they are imprisoned by malicious wizards or beset by seductive enchantresses, agents of evil, bent upon the downfall of the Round Table. Gawain's reception suggests the former (807–900). It is as though he had arrived at another Camelot, a world of ordered ceremony where everyone, from the *porter pure pleasaunt* to the servants who kneel to welcome him, the knights and squires who conduct him to the hall, and the lord who makes him free of all the castle contains, is actuated by punctilious courtesy. Everything there is in sharp contrast with the frozen, wintry world outside; within the security of its welcoming walls he is stripped of his armour, dressed in soft garments glowing with the bright colours of spring, and set down to feast before a blazing fire. He finds himself amongst men who know how to value him for what he is (901–27): no sooner have they learnt his name than they crowd into his presence, anxious to observe in a renowned courtier the most delicate practice of courtesy. In this decent Christian household he is able to fulfil his religious duties, as he had longed to do upon the road, and at evensong on Christmas Eve he meets the ladies of the castle, one young and beautiful, the other old and ugly yet honoured by all about her (928–94). With them and the lord he passes the festive season with all the pleasures of the previous Christmas at Camelot, and no thought of his mission until he is about to depart; but the lord detains him, telling him that his goal, the Green Chapel, is not two miles off, and Gawain gratefully agrees to stay until New Year's morning (995–1104).

The second section of the poem is almost at an end, and for hundreds of lines nothing significant seems to have occurred. The conventional romance is action-packed, and though it may pause to describe a feast or to pursue a subsidiary episode the plot is not allowed to stagnate. Here, though the reader may surmise from the detail in which she is first described that the lord's wife is to play an important role, noting the enthusiasm with which Gawain greets her and how often they are together during the festivities, and though he may be puzzled by the equal prominence of the elder lady, for whom romance tradition suggests no obvious role, and by the almost frenetic activity of the lord in stirring up Christmas sports, he will detect no onward development of the plot. And he is unlikely to attach much importance to the last of the Christmas sports, a jocular compact proposed by the lord—and sealed in drink—that he and his guest should exchange what they gain on each of the three following days, he in the hunting field, Gawain in the castle (1105–25). Having put himself under his host's command for the festive season, Gawain cannot refuse without discourtesy; but such sporting compacts are the very stuff of romance and he shows no reluctance to accept it as such: '"if you are pleased to sport so, I am perfectly content"'. It apparently awakens no memories of an earlier compact for an equal exchange which turned out to be much more than a Christmas game.

III

The third section, in contrast to the casual sequence of the second, is highly structured, if—at first sight—just as irrelevant to the basic plot. On each of the last three days of the old year the same pattern is repeated: the lord and his followers go hunting, while Gawain is visited in his bedroom by the lady, who presses her attentions upon him. By employing all the social skills of chivalry he avoids any offence either to her or to her husband, to whom each evening he pays over the kisses she has given him in return for the spoils of the hunt. This structural parallelism suggests thematic implications, and there is an obvious relationship between the lord's hunting and the lady's amorous pursuit of Gawain. But the former is, in the medieval view, a natural fulfilment of man's role in nature and should end in the death of his prey. Can the latter also have such fundamental significance and such dire implications?

If so, they are concealed by a persistent atmosphere of comedy. The opening of the first bedroom scene (1178–318) is characteristic:

Gawain, naked in his bed, embarrassed by the sight of his host's wife stealing into the room, more embarrassed still when she sits down on the bed, feigning sleep, debating with himself as to her intentions, miming surprise when at last he 'wakens', is a comic figure—and one with whom all men can sympathise, regardless of the centuries and their changing social codes. Suddenly he is no longer the stereotyped hero of romance, the knight in shining armour, but a fellow being—man the hunter hunted by his prey—whose dilemma we can appreciate all the more sharply as our relieved laughter recognises that *we* are not the hunted. For the medieval reader this detached sympathy would be heightened by the realisation that Gawain's dilemma springs partly from his own reputation; from that aspect of it symbolised by the embroidered *vrysoun* about his helmet (608–14)[5]—so casually associated with the moral symbolism of armour and heraldic device—his reputation as a perfect practitioner of courtly love-making, renowned for his amorous conquests. It was for this, as much as his chivalric renown, that the members of the lord's household had welcomed him on arrival (910–27); and it is of this that the lady persistently reminds him: '"there are many ladies who would rather have you, dear sir, in their power now, as I have you here, to exchange pleasantries in delightful conversation with you, find solace for themselves and assuage their longings …"'

For a moment Gawain is baffled, unsure of himself, as he tries to identify this beautiful creature who tucks the bedclothes around him and claims him as her prisoner. Is she one of those seductive enchantresses who lie in wait in the pages of romance to ensnare knights? If so, the sign of the cross will cause her to vanish in a puff of smoke. Or is she what she seems to be, his host's wife, seduced by his reputation, offering him her body (1237–40)?[6] If so, how should he respond? Once again he is faced by a challenger whose nature is ambiguous. And once again he falls back upon the chivalric code and seeks refuge in punctilious courtesy: taking her ambivalent offer at its innocent, superficial level and echoing the language of courtly love poetry in which she claims him as her prisoner, he contrives to make the affair a game, a verbal contest in the *luf-talkyng* for which he is so renowned—gently reminding the lady that she has a husband (1268–79) while declaring himself, in the conventional formula, her knight. Only when she challenges his very identity, denying that he is Gawain

5 See the note on these lines below.

6 See the note on these lines below.

'"in whom courtliness is so completely embodied"', does he consent to a kiss at parting. And that he duly surrenders to his host at the end of the day (1372–401), amidst knowing jests which imply the husband's complicity, but in a light-hearted way as ambiguous as the interview with his wife and also, therefore, possibly innocent, possibly not.

Next day, while the lord hunts the boar (1412–67, 1561–618), the lady returns to the attack (1468–557): 'she was with him very early to get him to change his attitude'. She begins where she had left off: Gawain having once allowed himself to be kissed, she chooses to assume his agreement to her dictum that kissing *bicumes vche a knyȝt þat cortaysy vses*. She goes on to interpret all chivalry in terms of *þe lel layk of luf*: '"in all the records of chivalric conduct, the thing most praised is the faithful practice of love, the gospel of the knightly profession"'. It is an interpretation which the values of conventional romance might support, but not those associated with the perfect pentangle: Gawain, without being self-consciously moralistic, cannot forget his personal  *clannes* nor his *felaȝschyp* to the lady's husband. Interpreting *cortaysye* in balanced relationship with the other components of his *trawþe*, he confines it to verbal forms which, without offending, yet yield nothing: 'he defended himself so skilfully that no offence was apparent, nor any impropriety on either side'. In keeping with which he accepts two kisses and, faithful to his bargain, passes them on to his host at the close of the day (1619–47).

On the third day, while the lord hunts the fox (1690–732, 1893–923), the challenge is renewed more keenly still (1733–872): 'For that noble princess pressed him so hard, urging him so near to the limit, that he must needs either accept her love there and then, or refuse offensively; he was concerned for his courtesy, lest he should behave like a boor, and even more for his plight if he should commit a sin, and be a traitor to the man who owned that castle.' With all possible delicacy he insists that he can have no sweetheart at present. It is a conventional excuse—the preoccupation of a knight on a mission—but the lady accepts it, admits defeat and rises to leave. If her wooing represented any threat it is, apparently, at an end. At parting she asks for a trifle, a glove perhaps, as a keepsake; but a glove might be displayed as a love token and Gawain makes a polite excuse, rejecting in turn a ring which the lady wishes to give him and then her own green girdle. But she presses the girdle upon him, telling him that it has the power to protect the wearer from death. Throughout the Christmas festivities death has never been far from Gawain's mind: the thought of the blow to come distracts him from the lady's beauty (1283–7), he begs leave to set out for the Green Chapel even before the three days of the compact are over (1668–71), and his sleep is troubled by dreams of the fate that awaits him there (1750–4). And so now 'it occurred to him that it would be a godsend for the perilous adventure which was assigned him: if, when he came to the chapel to meet his doom, he managed to escape being slain, it would be an excellent device'. He accepts the girdle and, in obedience to the lady's urging 'loyally to keep it from her husband', makes no mention of it that evening when he presents him with the three kisses won during the day (1924–51). The compact has been kept, the lady's advances resisted; the light-hearted Christmas interlude is at an end, and Gawain is ready to face the real threat which lies ahead of him.

Earlier on this last day Gawain has made the final, vitally important preparation by going to confession, where 'he confessed himself fully and laid bare his sins, both big and small, imploring forgiveness, and begging the priest for absolution; and he absolved him fully and made him as pure as if Judgement Day were to fall upon the following day'. A valid confession requires three things: contrition for sins committed, restitution of anything wrongfully acquired, and resolution to sin no more. But from the moment when Gawain 'put away the love-lace the lady had given him, hiding it very carefully where he could find it later', his intention to make restitution has been in doubt. The confession which follows, outwardly wholly sincere, can only appear ambiguous until Gawain's silence regarding the girdle at the nightly exchange of winnings makes clear what his intention had always been. Without restitution the confession is invalid. In retrospect, this outcome has been inevitable from the moment when Gawain promised the lady not to surrender the girdle to her husband; to have done so would have been a breach of *cortaysye* towards her, yet to retain it is a breach of *felaȝschyp* towards her lord. These social lapses might be regarded as merely venial, offences against chivalry rather than mortal sins, but the symbolism of the pentangle unites code and faith indissolubly. Further, by coveting the girdle (which rightly belongs to the lord) Gawain has sinned against *fraunchyse*, and, by his false confession, against spiritual purity (*clannes*) and Christian duty (*pité*). In sum, he is guilty of *untrawþe*; his perfect pentangle is fatally flawed. And, ironically, he seems quite unconscious of any defect, enjoying himself on the last evening so thoroughly that others comment, '"Indeed, he has never before been in such high spirits since he came here."'

How can Gawain, whose pentangle proclaims high moral idealism, have fallen into such error? The poet makes no comment, but he has, perhaps, provided a guide to understanding, though at a superficial level, in Gawain's behaviour when the lady first enters his bedroom: 'the knight was embarrassed, and lay down artfully and pretended to be asleep'. The reaction is instantaneous, instinctive; but it puts Gawain in a false position from which he can only extract himself by acting out a white lie, making use, as he starts up in affected surprise, of the sign of the cross with which, elsewhere in the poem, he invokes divine aid in serious peril. The misuse of the sacred symbol passes unnoticed in the comedy of the scene, comedy rooted in the contrast between the knight's exalted reputation and the natural humanity of his behaviour. His retention of the green girdle is equally understandable in human terms: with death facing him next day, an apparent means of escape offers itself, he snatches at it instinctively—and falls prey to the temptress whom he has so long eluded by every wily shift in his power. And at that moment, far away in the forest, another hunt comes to an end: the artful fox, having evaded the hounds all day, has them hard on his heels when suddenly the lord appears in his path with drawn sword; he starts back instinctively and falls into the mouths of his pursuers. The hunt, whose thematic parallel to the temptation has been pleasantly remote while its atmosphere of natural, outdoor activity contrasts agreeably with the unnatural pursuit of male by female going on indoors, suddenly becomes acutely relevant, the fox's end suggesting a fateful paradox: he who seeks to save his life shall lose it. But Gawain, unconscious that the lord's gift of the fox skin is a *memento mori*, goes to bed secure in his possession of the girdle and conscious of absolution—though for him Judgement Day is to fall upon the following day.

IV

Doomsday dawns wild and stormy, the cold reality of nature obtruding upon the sheltered world of light and warmth where—to all outward appearances—Gawain has lain snug and safe throughout the Christmas festivities. But now a new year is beginning and the knight cannot sleep, reminded by every crowing cock that the fateful day has come (1998–2008). Springing up, he is dressed and armed in a miniature version of the arming scene at Arthur's court, recalling its ritual significance (2009–24). But there is an ironic addition to his equipment: over the surcoat bearing his heraldic device, symbol of his *trawþe*, he ties the green girdle, symbol of his *untrawþe* (2025–46).[7] Outwardly functional and conventional, the arming scene is full of ambiguities. Of what use will arms be under the Green Knight's axe? What moral value or protective power can the pentangle have, worn in conjunction with that other talisman, the girdle, dishonestly obtained? Why is the latter called a love token (*drurye*)?—though it may have been offered as such, it was certainly not accepted out of love. The poet provides no answers. Instead he assures us that Gawain did not wear the girdle for its material value—who would suppose that he did?—'but to protect himself, when he had to submit to facing death without resisting or defending himself with sword or dagger'. But will it? the mind asks, all the more anxiously because—outwardly at least—Gawain seems serenely untroubled by doubt. Which was, presumably, the poet's intention in planting so many ambiguities.

There is a similarly ironic disparity between the reader's and the hero's points of view as Gawain praises the hospitality shown him and, commending the castle to Christ, crosses himself and rides away (2047–74). He is guided on the way by a member of the household, who gives him a terrifying description of the guardian of the Green Chapel, massive, malicious, preying on all who pass, knight, priest or peasant. The guide urges Gawain to abandon his mission and escape, promising to conceal the fact, but the knight refuses and his companion leaves him (2074–159). Once again Gawain has met with a tempter and been challenged to choose between cowardice and death; once again his choice is complicated by ambiguities. The guide's description of the Green Knight develops one aspect of the ambivalent figure who appeared at Arthur's court, ignoring the courtly, ironic challenger but extending and darkening his Wild Man characteristics until, as slayer of all three social orders, he seems like Death himself. But here amongst the snow, in the harsh light of day, Gawain shows none of the uncertainty which troubled him within the castle in face of the lady's wiles. Calmly and courteously he rejects temptation and rides on in confidence: '"I will not weep or moan; I am wholly obedient to God's will, and have committed myself utterly to him"'—seeing no irony in that 'utterly', apparently unconscious of the girdle about his waist.

His confidence receives a rude shock when he comes within sight of the Green Chapel (2160–96). Whatever he had expected, whatever the name might suggest to the medieval imagination familiar with the wayside chapels of romance where erring knights confess to helpful

7 See the note on lines 2025–9 below.

hermits, the reality is entirely unexpected: *nobot an olde caue, / Or a creuisse of an olde cragge.* As a chapel the natural structure is profoundly unnatural; Gawain, his equanimity shaken, senses the perversity of the place: '"it is the Devil who has imposed this tryst on me in order to destroy me here; this is a chapel of doom"'. His nerves are further assaulted by the harsh grinding noise, as of a scythe being sharpened, which bursts from the rock above his head (2197–211), but he conceals the doubts in his heart under a bold exterior—and the more aware we become of the troubled heart the more our sympathies are drawn to the man. His challenging shout is answered by the Green Knight, who, his head restored, appears as at Arthur's court, but now on his own ground, in his natural setting (2212–46). They proceed to the return blow (2247–313), Gawain coolly exposing his neck—'he would not tremble with terror'. At the first feint he shrinks slightly and is rebuked for cowardice, then endures unflinching a second feint which enrages him, and finally a blow which just grazes his neck, severing the skin. The triple test is over, the challenger's stratagem has somehow failed, Gawain is saved; and as he sees his own blood gleam on the snow, he leaps back ready to defend himself, a free knight once again (2313–30). The dilemma has resolved itself in the best manner of romance; a challenge resolutely faced to the brink of death has proved a figment and we can rejoice with the hero: 'never since his mother bore him had he ever been half so happy as then'.

But the blow is still to fall—indeed, a rain of blows. They come in the words of the Green Knight (2331–68), who explains that the three feints just offered relate to the three days of the exchange-of-winnings compact and that the trifling wound is punishment for retaining the girdle, a failure in honesty, for 'an honest man must make honest reparation'. Gawain is stunned, racked by shame and mortification, his knightly self-control shattered; tearing off the girdle, he throws it back at the Green Knight (2369–88). He is answered by laughter—laughter in which we may see the ambivalent character of the Green Knight, challenger in a life-and-death contest, fuse with that of the lord, Sir Bertilak, jovial proposer of a Christmas game. Now he is cast in a new role by the terms in which Gawain phrases his bitter self-accusation: '"Because I feared your blow, cowardice led me to have to do with covetousness, to forsake my true nature, that generosity and fidelity which is proper to knights. Now I am lacking in fidelity and guilty of breach of faith, I who have always abhorred treachery and dishonesty … I here humbly confess to you, sir, that my behaviour is very sinful;

let me understand your pleasure with respect to penance, and henceforth I will be on my guard.'" As if with a blinding flash of insight Gawain has correctly identified the nature of his offence against chivalric principles and personal integrity and admits it frankly. But the terms he uses acknowledge, consciously or unconsciously, a much more profound error, his imperfect confession to the priest in Bertilak's castle. His confession to Bertilak, a layman, cannot bring formal absolution but it displays the essential prerequisites of contrition and resolution not to sin again. As Gawain has already made restitution of the girdle and done penance under the Green Knight's axe, his 'confessor' responds unhesitatingly: "'I consider you absolved of that offence and purged as clean as if you had never sinned since the day you were born.'"

Bertilak's acceptance of the role of confessor implies knowledge of Gawain's guilty secret, and his identity is now more mysterious than ever. But his laughter, the ironic humour with which he returns the girdle, green as himself, to Gawain as a memento of the adventure of the Green Chapel—tying together, without comment, the challenge and temptation episodes—and his invitation to return to his castle and be reconciled with his wife, "'who was your keen opponent'", bring a relaxation of tension (2389–406); the affair is at an end. But not for Gawain. Bitterly he inveighs against both the ladies in the castle "'who have so cleverly deceived their knight with their trickery'", against the sex in general, responsible for the downfall of many great and wise men, Solomon amongst them, and against himself as a fool brought to grief through the wiles of women (2407–38). He accepts the girdle, but as a badge of dishonour, "'to remind myself with remorse of the sinfulness and the frailty of the erring flesh, how liable it is to catch the plague spots of sin'". His persistence in treating the issue as a serious moral one appears increasingly at variance with the conventional romance conclusion as Bertilak reveals the underlying motivation of the adventure, the traditional enmity of the enchantress Morgan le Fay towards Arthur's court (2439–70).

The challenge, then, had been to the reputation of the Round Table as a whole; but to Gawain his failure is personal and inexcusable. Refusing Bertilak's invitation, he returns to Arthur's court and, with shame and mortification, proclaims his fault (2471–512): "'See! my lord," said the knight, touching the girdle, "this is the blazon of this guilty scar I bear in my neck, this is the badge of the injury and the harm which I have received because of the cowardice and covetousness to which I there fell prey'". The situation is conventional: his adventures safely concluded, the hero displays before his fellow knights the trophies gained. The outcome, however, is not the conventional reaffirmation of chivalric values but the bitter self-indictment of a defeated and humiliated man, a disappointed idealist who has fallen short of his own absolute standards. He has already implicitly rejected the more tolerant judgement of his opponent, who accepts relative standards and the limitations of human nature: '"as a pearl in comparison with a dried pea is of greater value, so, truthfully, is Gawain beside other gallant knights. Yet in this you were a little at fault, sir, and lacking in fidelity; but that was not for any excellence of workmanship in the girdle, nor because of wooing either, but because you loved your life; I blame you the less for that."' It is from the judgement of his peers that Gawain must expect confirmation of his values. Their response is laughter and immediate agreement that the whole court should wear the green girdle (2513–21): 'For the good repute of the Round Table was associated with it, and ever afterwards anyone who wore it was honoured, as is written in the best books of romance.'

How is this response to be interpreted? Is the laughter an echo of the Green Knight's indulgent understanding of human frailty or of the court's own *rechles* mirth before—and after—his challenge to the reputation of their society? Will they wear the green girdle lightly as a chivalric trophy, the badge of an adventure achieved; or, like Gawain, as a penitential token, reminder of a lesson learnt? The reader must decide for himself in the light of whatever opinion he has already formed of the court's sincerity and good judgement. Superficially their response is perfectly in keeping with 'the best books of romance', and the poem has no comment to make upon it, except by echoing as it ends (2522–8) the opening lines, with their reminder of the place of Arthurian story in human history and of the ambivalence of personal reputation and social values. If the reader now sees much more than a conventional formula in these lines, he may reflect that, though the life of the individual is linear, the life of the race is cyclic and mankind may learn from experience. And, making his own judgement on chivalric values and human perfectibility, he may echo the poet's closing prayer to the Victor crowned with a symbol of defeat and shame (2529–30): 'now may He who wore the crown of thorns bring us to His bliss!'

But what does it all mean? The conventional romance normally offers definitive solutions to specific questions: the supreme chivalric virtue is ——; great love inspires the greatest chivalry; spiritual chivalry is greater than temporal chivalry. But here there are no absolutes and a whole series of interrelated queries is left with the reader. Can he accept the court's judgement on Gawain's adventure, with its implication that in chivalry ends justify means and honour exists in the eyes of the world rather than the heart of the individual? If so, he must see the romance as purely conventional, somewhat unsatisfactory in outcome but innocent of ironies or ambiguities. If not, can he agree with Gawain's bitter self-denunciation and accept the implications for lesser mortals like himself of the failure of one who aspired to perfect chivalry? Or has the poet persuaded him to see the hero, trapped between conflicting aspects of his chivalric reputation, as an all too human comic figure? Alternatively, does he agree with Sir Bertilak that there is no dishonour in responding to the human instinct for self-preservation and accept that relative rather than absolute success is all that even the best of mortals can achieve? Whatever he decides, the richly organised subject-matter and undogmatic presentation should encourage him to pursue any thematic repercussions raised in his mind. The fourteenth-century reader might be led to consider the nature of contemporary romance, the decadence of a form in which a noble and valid idealism was being increasingly trivialised by the repetitive, formulaic situations posed, the glib, contrived solutions, and the ever-widening gap between ordinary human experience and the behaviour, not of the supernatural testing agents, licensed by tradition, but of the chivalric heroes. This in turn could lead him to re-examine an idealism which, however perfectly it functioned in the black-and-white world of romance, where good and evil assume traditional forms, might be an inadequate guide amongst the half-tones of everyday life, where the enemy within often goes unrecognised and instinct and moral sense may be unconsciously opposed. The result, for the modern as for the medieval reader, need not be a rejection of all codes but a heightened awareness of the balance to be kept between idealism and realism in all human aspirations. The need for self-awareness, both in the individual and in society as a whole, may imply the importance of tradition and literature in the self-education of mankind, raising in turn the whole issue of the relation of literature to life.

But if the poem means so much, why does it not speak more openly? Why so many ambiguities, so much irony? Working within a long-established tradition and probably under direct patronage, the *Gawain* poet had much less liberty than the modern author to select his own audience by addressing himself to those members of the general reading public who might welcome innovations. Recognising the challenge, he has responded creatively, making merits of its difficulties. He has fulfilled his professional obligation by providing an acceptable example of a familiar form, exploiting its conventions with intimate understanding. But recognising the limitations of the form and the ability of some of his readers to transcend them, he has worked through the romance medium to widen and deepen the conventional means of expression. To have worked against it would merely have alienated his patrons. Instead he has made them his collaborators, constantly thrusting upon them the responsibility of deciding, interpreting, understanding. The material he provides is detailed, clear, concrete, often deceptively so. But is the Green Knight man or ogre? Can Gawain's confession be valid? Is honour relative or absolute? If the reader is lulled into passivity by the familiarity of the form, or if his thinking is purely conventional, he will be jerked to attention by the shocks which await the conscientious, punctiliously correct but somewhat conventional hero. The ambiguities are there to alert him, the ironies to guide him; he may miss them at a first reading, but the cyclic form of the poem invites reflection and re-reading. At each reading the structural and thematic complexities become more apparent, the ambiguities more richly harmonised, the verbal patterns more clearly intentional; new overtones of meaning emerge, a process of discovery seemingly limited only by the reader's sensitivity. The meaning is rooted not in code or convention but in humanity, so that to an age for which chivalry is dead it still has something to say of man's aspirations and limitations, of moral scrupulosity and self-blindness, of the sense of honour and the sense of humour. That is why *Sir Gawain and the Green Knight* is a classic and why a translation, however inadequate, is worth attempting.

Guide to further reading

The Introduction to this edition of *Sir Gawain and the Green Knight* gives only an outline reading. There is much more to the poem, as readers will observe for themselves. The thematic balance of idealism and realism can only be individually determined; the complexity and ambiguity invite and license interpretation. The academic response, a flood of books and papers, has sometimes been unhelpful to students, partly because of its sheer bulk and diversity. But also because there has been a tendency to base overall readings on extraneous factors, mythical or anthropological, or on the interpretation of a particular symbol or pattern of incidents. Recently, however, a general consensus has emerged which is being progressively refined, successive studies adding overtones of meaning to an increasingly harmonised understanding.

Date, dialect, author, audience

Despite objections that the dating of the poem to the last ten or fifteen years of the fourteenth century rests on details of armour and equipment which would not preclude an earlier date of composition, such evidence does not offer conclusive proof of any earlier date. Equally, though the area of composition has been more narrowly defined as the Cheshire/Staffordshire border and a number of individuals identified as possible authors of the poem—most notably, perhaps, John Massy of Cotton in east Cheshire, a Lancastrian retainer—no name, as yet, commands general acceptance. Those named tend to be adherents of notable Staffordshire or Cheshire families, reopening the long-standing issue of the contrast between the supposed provincial origin of the poem and its manifest courtliness and sophistication. Attention has been drawn in Michael J. Bennett, *Community, Class and Careerism: Cheshire and Lancashire Society in the Age of 'Sir Gawain and the Green Knight'* (Cambridge, 1983) to the presence at court during the later reign of Richard II of a large group of Cheshire notables. A more general study of the social and cultural context in which the poem was produced is provided in Elizabeth Salter, *Fourteenth Century English Poetry: Contexts and Readings* (Oxford, 1983). Investigation continues of the implications of a London audience, including the city merchants whose mercantile values have been detected in fusion with the chivalric idealism of the poem, perhaps underestimating the difficulties which the complex alliteration and regional vocabulary of *Sir Gawain* would present to a metropolitan audience and exaggerating the cultural gap separating royal and provincial courts between which many nobles divided their time.

Sources

The issue of sources has undergone a similar redefinition; where it was once understood in terms of plot components it is now loosely interpreted as random motifs and incidents paralleled in a wide range of French romances. The limitations of the search for narrative analogues to a work in which plot is no more than a framework are clearly demonstrated in Elizabeth Brewer, *'Sir Gawain and the Green Knight': Sources and Analogues* (2nd edn, Cambridge, 1992). The new approach underlies Ad Putter, *'Sir Gawain and the Green Knight' and French Arthurian Romance* (Oxford, 1995), in which comparative analysis of the romances of Chrétien de Troyes and his continuators and contemporaries demonstrates the intellectual and literary climate out of which *Sir Gawain* was written, without, in general, implying direct borrowing of specific incidents or episodes. Much remains to be done in this field: the poet's reading was no doubt wider than so far demonstrated and his use of established conventions and motifs distinctive and creative, challenging the audience's judgement as to how their conventional meaning has been varied in the process.

Interpretation

The basic interpretative study remains John A. Burrow, *A Reading of 'Sir Gawain and the Green Knight'* (London, 1965), though its interpretation has been extended, qualified and, in some points, contradicted by more recent work. Attention has been drawn in Derek Brewer, *Symbolic Stories: Traditional Narratives of the Family Drama in English Literature* (Cambridge, 1980) to the extent to which traditional themes and structures of folktale underlie the procedures of medieval romance, though not everyone would accept the interpretation of *Sir Gawain* implied. Among the earlier readings, that in Donald R. Howard, *The Three Temptations: Medieval Man in Search of the World* (Princeton, 1966) interprets the hero's failure in terms of the conflict between Christian ideology and the secular idealism of chivalry. In W. R. J. Barron,

'Trawthe' and Treason: The Sin of Gawain Reconsidered (Manchester, 1980) these are seen as complementary values integrated in the figure of the pentangle, symbol of *trawthe*, and Gawain's fault as a breach of both, metaphorically implied in the interrelation of the bedroom and the hunting scenes, each hunt ending with a different version of the penalty for treason, relating Gawain to the archetypal traitor Aeneas. A similar duality is at the core of Victor Y. Haines, *The Fortunate Fall of Sir Gawain: The Typology of 'Sir Gawain and the Green Knight'* (Washington, 1982), in which his fault is equated with the *felix culpa* of Adam which brought redemption for mankind, a thematic interpretation mirrored in the moral seriousness and high comedy of the poem.

A group of studies based on the interpretative application of medieval academic and theological conceptions includes R. A. Shoaf, *The Poem as Green Girdle: 'Commercium' in 'Sir Gawain and the Green Knight'* (Gainesville, 1984), which analyses the commercial vocabulary of the poem as reflecting contemporary theological speculation about the sacraments and relates it to the issue of Gawain's covetousness. Similarly, Ross G. Arthur, *Medieval Sign Theory and 'Sir Gawain and the Green Knight'* (Toronto, 1987) relates medieval teaching on symbols to the poet's use of pentangle, girdle, etc. to provoke a meditation on the difficulties of spiritually productive reading. And Gerald Morgan, *'Sir Gawain and the Green Knight' and the Idea of Righteousness* (Blackrock, 1991) uses scholastic philosophy to explain how Gawain's fault can be reconciled with his virtues.

The key interpretative crux remains the nature of that fault—chivalric, in failing to fulfil the exchange agreement with Bertilak, or spiritual, arising from the nature of the confession made at Hautdesert—and, if the latter, its degree, mortal or venial. The ambiguity of the poetic method may suggest that the poet's intention was not to create a mystery story with a single, concealed solution but to provoke the reader to personal exploration of a moral maze. Wendy Clein, *Concepts of Chivalry in 'Sir Gawain and the Green Knight'* (Norman, 1987) focuses on the indeterminate ending of the poem, particularly the conflicting evaluation of Gawain's behaviour, to suggest that the intention was to stimulate consideration of the cultural ideas involved, in particular the meaning of chivalry and death.

Literary art

The general literary context of *Sir Gawain* in English Arthurian literature is described and analysed in W. R. J. Barron, ed., *The Arthur of the English* (Cardiff, 1998). The basic book on the art of the poem is Larry D. Benson, *Art and Tradition in 'Sir Gawain and the Green Knight'* (New Brunswick, 1965), which demonstrates the poet's skill in making use of all the traditional elements available to him—the established associations of plot components, the conventions of romance, his stylistic inheritance—for his particular purpose. The more technical aspects of his medium are exhaustively analysed in Marie Borroff, *'Sir Gawain and the Green Knight': A Stylistic and Metrical Study* (New Haven, 1962). A less technical, literary-critical approach to the poet's creativity informs the work of A. C. Spearing, *The 'Gawain'-Poet: A Critical Study* (Cambridge, 1970). A similar analysis of all four poems attributed to him, focusing in particular on themes and characterisation, is W. A. Davenport, *The Art of the 'Gawain'-Poet* (London, 1978), while in Edmund Wilson, *The 'Gawain'-Poet* (Leiden, 1976) many points of detail in all four are used to illustrate the intellectual and philological resources of the poet. Characteristic of the increasingly detailed appreciation of the poet's creative method is Sarah Stanbury, *Seeing the 'Gawain'-Poet: Description and the Act of Perception* (Philadelphia, 1991), which analyses the extensive vocabulary of seeing in the poem as an approach to the descriptive element and the use of 'point of view' in the narrative, as an adjunct to its themes of moral choice and of variant judgement on the evidence of the senses.

Collections of scholarship

Many advances in our understanding of *Sir Gawain* come piecemeal in scholarly papers, a selection of which is conveniently accessible in the following publications:

Blanch, Robert J., ed., *'Sir Gawain and the Green Knight' and 'Pearl': Critical Essays* (Bloomington, 1966)

Fox, Denton, ed., *Twentieth Century Interpretations of 'Sir Gawain and the Green Knight': A Collection of Critical Essays* (Englewood Cliffs, 1968)

Howard, Donald R., and Christian Zacher, eds, *Critical Studies of 'Sir Gawain and the Green Knight'* (Notre Dame, 1968)

Blanch, Robert J., M. Y. Miller and J. N. Wasserman, eds, *Text and Matter: New Critical Perspectives on the 'Pearl'-Poet* (Troy, NY, 1991)

Brewer, Derek, and Jonathan Gibson, eds, *A Companion to the 'Gawain'-Poet* (Cambridge, 1997)

Bibliographies

Andrew, Malcolm, *The 'Gawain'-Poet: An Annotated Bibliography 1839–1977* (New York, 1979)

Stainsby, Meg, *'Sir Gawain and the Green Knight': An Annotated Bibliography 1978–89* (New York, 1992)

Bibliographical Bulletin of the International Arthurian Society (annual volumes)

Sir Gawain
and the Green Knight

I

Siþen þe sege and þe assaut watȝ sesed at Troye,
Þe borȝ brittened and brent to brondeȝ and askeȝ,
Þe tulk þat þe trammes of tresoun þer wroȝt
Watȝ tried for his tricherie, þe trewest on erthe.
Hit watȝ Ennias þe athel, and his highe kynde,
Þat siþen depreced prouinces, and patrounes bicome
Welneȝe of al þe wele in þe west iles.
Fro riche Romulus to Rome ricchis hym swyþe,
With gret bobbaunce þat burȝe he biges vpon fyrst,
And neuenes hit his aune nome, as hit now hat;
Ticius to Tuskan and teldes bigynnes,
Langaberde in Lumbardie lyftes vp homes,
And fer ouer þe French flod Felix Brutus
On mony bonkkes ful brode Bretayn he setteȝ
wyth wynne,
Where werre and wrake and wonder
Bi syþeȝ hatȝ wont þerinne,
And oft boþe blysse and blunder
Ful skete hatȝ skyfted synne.

Ande quen þis Bretayn watȝ bigged bi þis burn rych,
Bolde bredden þerinne, baret þat lofden,
In mony turned tyme tene þat wroȝten.
Mo ferlyes on þis folde han fallen here oft
Þen in any oþer þat I wot, syn þat ilk tyme.
Bot of alle þat here bult of Bretaygne kynges
Ay watȝ Arthur þe hendest, as I haf herde telle;
Forþi an aunter in erde I attle to schawe,
Þat a selly in siȝt summe men hit holden,
And an outtrage awenture of Arthureȝ wondereȝ;
If ȝe wyl lysten þis laye bot on littel quile,
I schal telle hit as-tit, as I in toun herde,
with tonge;
As hit is stad and stoken
In stori stif and stronge,
With lel letteres loken,
In londe so hatȝ ben longe.

I

After the siege and the assault had ended at Troy, and the city had been broken down and burnt to charred beams and ashes, the man who wove the web of treason there was tried for his deceit, yet famed as the truest of men. It was the prince Aeneas, and his noble race, who later conquered other kingdoms, and became the lords of almost all the wealth in the lands to the west. When the mighty Romulus has quickly made his way to Rome, straightway he builds that city with great magnificence, and names it with his own name, as it is still called; Ticius goes to Tuscany and founds settlements, Langobard raises homesteads in Lombardy, and far away across the English Channel Felix Brutus on many a broad hill happily establishes Britain, where from age to age there have been wars and reprisals, marvels and atrocities, and where triumphs and disasters have constantly and quickly succeeded one another ever since.

And when this Britain had been founded by that prince of men, a bold race was bred there, lovers of strife, who in many a troubled age made mischief. In this land greater wonders have repeatedly occurred than in any other that I know of, ever since that time. But of all who dwelt here as kings of Britain, Arthur, as I've heard tell, was the noblest ever. And so I mean to reveal an actual occurrence, such that some men consider it a veritable marvel, and an extraordinary episode from the strange tales of Arthur. If you will listen to this lay for just a little while, I will recite it here and now, as I have heard it told, and as it is recorded and set down in a bold and powerful story, expressed in truthful words, as it has long been in this land.

Þis kyng lay at Camylot vpon Krystmasse,
With mony luflych lorde, ledeȝ of þe best,
Rekenly of þe Rounde Table alle þo rich breþer,
With rych reuel oryȝt and rechles merþes.
Þer tournayed tulkes by tymeȝ ful mony;
Justed ful jolilé þise gentyle kniȝtes,
Syþen kayred to þe court, caroles to make.
For þer þe fest watȝ ilyche ful fiften dayes,
With alle þe mete and þe mirþe þat men couþe avyse;
Such glaum ande gle glorious to here,
Dere dyn vpon day, daunsyng on nyȝtes,
Al watȝ hap vpon heȝe in halleȝ and chambreȝ,
With lordeȝ and ladies, as leuest him þoȝt.
With all þe wele of þe worlde þay woned þer samen,
Þe most kyd knyȝteȝ vnder Krystes seluen,
And þe louelokkest ladies þat euer lif haden,
And he þe comlokest kyng þat þe court haldes.
For al watȝ þis fayre folk in her first age,
on sille,
Þe hapnest vnder heuen,
Kyng hyȝest mon of wylle;
Hit were now gret nye to neuen
So hardy a here on hille.

Wyle Nw Ȝer watȝ so ȝep þat hit watȝ nwe cummen,
Þat day doubble on þe dece watȝ þe douth serued.
Fro þe kyng watȝ cummen with knyȝtes into þe halle,
Þe chauntré of þe chapel cheued to an ende,
Loude crye watȝ þer kest of clerkeȝ and oþer,
Nowel nayted onewe, neuened ful ofte.
And syþen riche forth runnen to reche hondeselle,
Ȝeȝed ȝeres-ȝiftes on hiȝ, ȝelde hem bi hond.
Debated busyly aboute þo giftes;
Ladies laȝed ful loude, þoȝ þay lost haden,
And he þat wan watȝ not wrothe, þat may ȝe wel trawe.
Alle þis mirþe þay maden to þe mete tyme.
When þay had waschen worþyly, þay wenten to sete,
Þe best burne ay abof, as hit best semed.
Whene Guenore, ful gay, grayþed in þe myddes,
Dressed on þe dere des, dubbed al aboute,

The king was at Camelot at Christmas time, with many a handsome lord, the best of knights, all the noble brotherhood of the Round Table, duly assembled, with revels of fitting splendour and carefree pleasures. There they held tourney on many occasions; these noble knights jousted most gallantly, then rode back to the court to make merry. For there the celebrations went on continuously for fully fifteen days, with all the feasting and merry-making which could be devised; such sounds of mirth and merriment, glorious to hear, a pleasant uproar by day, dancing at night, nothing but the greatest happiness in halls and chambers, among lords and ladies, to their perfect contentment. With all the well-being in the world they dwelt there together, the most famous knights in Christendom, and the fairest ladies who ever lived, and he who held court there was the handsomest of kings. For this goodly company in the castle hall were all in the springtime of life, the most favoured on earth; their king the most noble-minded of men; it would now be very hard to name so valiant a company in any castle.

While New Year was so young that it had just newly arrived, on the day itself the company was served with redoubled splendour at table. When the king had come with his knights into the hall, the singing of Mass in the chapel having drawn to an end, a loud hubbub was raised there by clerics and others, Christmas was celebrated anew, 'Noel' called out again and again. And then nobles came forward to offer good-luck tokens, called aloud 'New Year gifts', proffered them in their hands. There was eager contention over the presents; ladies laughed loudly, even though they had lost, and he who won was not displeased, that you may well believe. They carried on all this merry-making until the dinner hour. When they had duly washed, they went to table, the noblest person always being more highly placed, as seemed most fitting. Queen Guenevere, brilliantly dressed, was set in the midst, placed on the dais of honour, all about her richly decorated, fine

Smal sendal bisides, a selure hir ouer
Of tryed tolouse, of tars tapites innoghe,
Þat were enbrawded and beten wyth þe best gemmes
Þat myȝt be preued of prys wyth penyes to bye,
in daye;
Þe comlokest to discrye
Þer glent with yȝen gray;
A semloker þat euer he syȝe
Soth moȝt no mon say.

Bot Arthure wolde not ete til al were serued,
He watȝ so joly of his joyfnes, and sumquat childgered:
His lif liked hym lyȝt, he louied þe lasse
Auþer to longe lye or to longe sitte,
So bisied him his ȝonge blod and his brayn wylde.
And also an oþer maner meued him eke,
Þat he þurȝ nobelay had nomen, he wolde neuer ete
Vpon such a dere day er hym deuised were
Of sum auenturus þyng an vncouþe tale,
Of sum mayn meruayle, þat he myȝt trawe,
Of alderes, of armes, of oþer auenturus,
Oþer sum segg hym bisoȝt of sum siker knyȝt
To joyne wyth hym in iustyng, in jopardé to lay,
Lede, lif for lyf, leue vchon oþer
As fortune wolde fulsun hom þe fayrer to haue.
Þis watȝ þe kynges countenaunce where he in court were,
At vch farand fest among his fre meny
in halle.
Þerfore of face so fere
He stiȝtleȝ stif in stalle,
Ful ȝep in þat Nw Ȝere,
Much mirthe he mas with alle.

Thus þer stondes in stale þe stif kyng hisseluen,
Talkkande bifore þe hyȝe table of trifles ful hende.
There gode Gawan watȝ grayþed Gwenore bisyde,
And Agrauayn a la dure mayn on þat oþer syde sittes,
Boþe þe kynges sistersunes and ful siker kniȝtes;

100 þe *supplied*

silk around her, a canopy above her of choice fabric of Toulouse, many hangings of Tharsian stuff, which were embroidered and set with the best gems that ever money could buy—the fairest jewel to be seen, her grey eyes shining; no man could truly say he ever saw a lovelier.

But Arthur would not eat until all had been served, he was so youthfully light-hearted, and rather boyish: he liked an active life, and was all the less willing either to lie idle or to sit still for long, his youthful blood and restless brain stirred him so. And he was also influenced by another custom, which he had assumed as a point of honour, that he would never eat upon such a festive day before he had been told a novel tale of some perilous incident, of some great wonder, which he could believe true, of princes of old, of feats of arms, or other adventurous deeds, or until someone had begged him for some trusty knight to join with him in jousting, a man ready to stake his life against another, each allowing the other such advantage as fortune should favour him with. This was the king's accustomed behaviour wherever he might be holding court, at every splendid feast among his noble company in castle hall. Therefore, proud of mien, he presides standing in his place, very youthful at that New Year, making much mirth with everyone.

And so the bold king in person stands in his place, talking graciously of this and that to those at the high table. There the good Sir Gawain is placed beside Guenevere, and Agravain of the Hard Hand sits on his other side, both nephews of the king and very worthy knights; Bishop

Bischop Bawdewyn abof biginez þe table,
And Ywan, Vryn son, ette with hymseluen.
Þise were diȝt on þe des and derworþly serued,
And siþen mony siker segge at þe sidbordez.
Þen þe first cors come with crakkyng of trumpes,
Wyth mony baner ful bryȝt þat þerbi henged;
Nwe nakryn noyse with þe noble pipes,
Wylde werbles and wyȝt wakned lote,
Þat mony hert ful hiȝe hef at her towches.
Dayntés dryuen þerwyth of ful dere metes,
Foysoun of þe fresche, and on so fele disches
Þat pine to fynde þe place þe peple biforne
For to sette þe sylueren þat sere sewes halden
        on clothe.
    Iche lede as he loued hymselue
    Þer laght withouten loþe;
    Ay two had disches twelue,
    Good ber and bryȝt wyn boþe.

Now wyl I of hor seruise say yow no more,
For vch wyȝe may wel wit no wont þat þer were.
An oþer noyse ful newe neȝed biliue,
Þat þe lude myȝt haf leue liflode to cach.
For vneþe watȝ þe noyce not a whyle sesed,
And þe fyrst cource in þe court kyndely serued,
Þer hales in at þe halle dor an aghlich mayster,
On þe most on þe molde on mesure hyghe;
Fro þe swyre to þe swange so sware and so þik,
And his lyndes and his lymes so longe and so grete,
Half etayn in erde I hope þat he were,
Bot mon most I algate mynn hym to bene,
And þat þe myriest in his muckel þat myȝt ride;
For of bak and of brest al were his bodi sturne,
Bot his wombe and his wast were worthily smale,
And alle his fetures folȝande in forme þat he hade,
        ful clene.
    For wonder of his hwe men hade,
    Set in his semblaunt sene;
    He ferde as freke were fade,
    And oueral enker-grene.

Bawdewyn, in the seat of honour, heads the table, and Ywain, Urien's son, dines beside him. They were seated on the dais and sumptuously served, and after them many trusty knights at the side tables. Then the first course came in with blaring of trumpets, from which hung many a bright banner; kettledrums burst into sound, with the splendid noise of pipes, wild warblings loudly wakened the echoes, so that many a heart was greatly uplifted by their strains. With that there came in rare dishes of the richest foods, fresh meat in plenty, and on so many plates that it was difficult to find room before the diners to set upon the cloth the silverware which held the various stews. Everyone there helped himself as he pleased, without stint; each couple had twelve dishes, good beer and bright wine as well.

Now I will tell you no more of how they were served, for everyone can well believe that there was nothing lacking. Another, quite different, sound quickly followed, so that the king might be free to take food. For scarcely had the sound of music ceased for an instant, and the first course been duly served in the court, when there comes dashing in at the door of the hall an awesome figure, quite the tallest in stature on this earth; from the neck to the waist so square-cut and so thick-set, and his loins and his arms and legs so long and so massive, that I believe he actually may have been half giant, but at any rate I declare he was the biggest of men, and yet the handsomest, for all his size, who ever bestrode a horse; for although his body—back and chest—was burly, yet his stomach and waist were becomingly slender, and all the features of his person were equally clean-cut. So that they were amazed at his colour, plain to see upon his countenance; he bore himself like a bold man and all over he was bright green.

Ande al grayþed in grene þis gome and his wedes:
A strayt cote ful streȝt, þat stek on his sides,
A meré mantile abof, mensked withinne
With pelure pured apert, þe pane ful clene
With blyþe blaunner ful bryȝt, and his hod boþe,
Þat watȝ laȝt fro his lokkeȝ and layde on his schulderes;
Heme wel-haled hose of þat same grene,
Þat spenet on his sparlyr, and clene spures vnder,
Of bryȝt golde, vpon silk bordes barred ful ryche,
And scholes vnder schankes þere þe schalk rides.
And alle his vesture uerayly watȝ clene verdure,
Boþe þe barres of his belt and oþer blyþe stones
Þat were richely rayled in his aray clene,
Aboutte hymself and his sadel, vpon silk werkeȝ.
Þat were to tor for to telle of tryfles þe halue
Þat were enbrauded abof, wyth bryddes and flyȝes,
With gay gaudi of grene, þe golde ay inmyddes.
Þe pendauntes of his payttrure, þe proude cropure,
His molaynes, and alle þe metail anamayld was þenne,
Þe steropes þat he stod on stayned of þe same,
And his arsounȝ al after and his aþel skyrtes,
Þat euer glemered and glent al of grene stones.
Þe fole þat he ferkkes on fyn of þat ilke,
sertayn:
A grene hors gret and þikke,
A stede ful stif to strayne,
In brawden brydel quik—
To þe gome he watȝ ful gayn.

Wel gay watȝ þis gome gered in grene,
And þe here of his hed of his hors swete:
Fayre fannand fax vmbefoldes his schulderes;
A much berd as a busk ouer his brest henges,
Þat wyth his hiȝlich here þat of his hed reches
Watȝ euesed al vmbetorne abof his elbowes,
Þat half his armes þervnder were halched in þe wyse
Of a kyngeȝ capados þat closes his swyre.
Þe mane of þat mayn hors much to hit lyke,
Wel cresped and cemmed, wyth knottes ful mony

171 skyrtes: MS sturtes

And everything about this man was green and his clothes were green: a straight tunic, very close-fitting, which clung to his sides, over it a gay mantle, adorned inside with close-trimmed fur, clearly visible, the facing resplendent with bright, pure white ermine, and his hood as well, which was thrown back from his locks and laid on his shoulders; neat, tight-drawn hose of the same green, which clung to his calves, and below, bright spurs of shining gold, on silk straps richly striped, and the man's feet, where they rest in the stirrups, were unshod. And his whole costume was, indeed, bright green, both the metal bars on his belt and various bright jewels which were richly disposed upon his elegant dress, about his person and his saddle, on silken embroidery. It would be too difficult to describe half the details that were embroidered upon it, with birds and butterflies, with bright ornaments of green, everywhere amongst the gold. The pendants of his horse's breast-harness, the splendid crupper, the studs on the bit, and all the metalwork was enamelled also, the stirrups in which he rested were coloured the same shade, and his saddle-bows and his magnificent saddle-skirts were just the same, continually gleaming and glinting all over with green jewels. Indeed, the horse that he rode on was of the same colour exactly: a great, stout green horse, a difficult beast to curb, restive in his embroidered bridle—yet he was perfectly obedient to the rider.

This man clothed in green was very fine, and the hair on his head matched that of his horse: handsome locks, fanning out to enfold his shoulders; a great bushy beard hanging down over his chest, which, together with the splendid hair falling from his head, was trimmed all round just above his elbows, so that his arms were half enclosed underneath it as if by the hooded cape of a king which fits closely about his neck. The mane of the massive horse was very similar to it, well curled and combed, with a great many ornamental knots plaited in

Folden in wyth fildore aboute þe fayre grene,
Ay a herle of þe here, an oþer of golde.
Þe tayl and his toppyng twynnen of a sute,
And bounden boþe wyth a bande of a bryȝt grene,
Dubbed wyth ful dere stoneȝ, as þe dok lasted,
Syþen þrawen wyth a þwong a þwarle knot alofte,
Þer mony belleȝ ful bryȝt of brende golde rungen.
Such a fole vpon folde, ne freke þat hym rydes,
Watȝ neuer sene in þat sale wyth syȝt er þat tyme,
with yȝe.
He loked as layt so lyȝt,
So sayd al þat hym syȝe;
Hit semed as no mon myȝt
Vnder his dyntteȝ dryȝe.

Wheþer hade he no helme ne hawbergh nauþer,
Ne no pysan ne no plate þat pented to armes,
Ne no schafte ne no schelde to schwue ne to smyte,
Bot in his on honde he hade a holyn bobbe,
Þat is grattest in grene when greueȝ ar bare,
And an ax in his oþer, a hoge and vnmete,
A spetos sparþe to expoun in spelle, quoso myȝt.
Þe lenkþe of an elnȝerde þe large hede hade,
Þe grayn al of grene stele and of golde hewen,
Þe bit burnyst bryȝt, with a brod egge
As wel schapen to schere as scharp rasores.
Þe stele of a stif staf þe sturne hit bi grypte,
Þat watȝ wounden wyth yrn to þe wandeȝ ende,
And al bigrauen with grene in gracios werkes;
A lace lapped aboute, þat louked at þe hede,
And so after þe halme halched ful ofte,
Wyth tryed tasseleȝ þerto tacched innoghe,
On botounȝ of þe bryȝt grene brayden ful ryche.
Þis haþel heldeȝ hym in and þe halle entres,
Driuande to þe heȝe dece, dut he no woþe;
Haylsed he neuer one, bot heȝe he ouer loked.
Þe fyrst word þat he warp, 'Wher is,' he sayd,
'Þe gouernour of þis gyng? Gladly I wolde
Se þat segg in syȝt, and with hymself speke
raysoun.'

210 lenkþe ... hede: MS hede ... lenkþe

with gold thread among the lovely green, always one strand of the hair and another of gold. The tail and his forelock were plaited to match, and both bound with a band of a vivid green, decorated with precious stones, to their cropped ends, then tied off by a thong with an intricate knot at the end, where many bright bells of pure gold tinkled. A real, living horse like that, and such a man as his rider, mortal eye had never set sight upon in that hall before that moment. His glance flashed bright as fire, so all who saw him said; it seemed as though no man could survive under blows from him.

Yet he had no helm nor hauberk either, and no gorget, nor any plate armour at all, and no spear or shield to thrust or parry with, but in one of his hands he had a spray of holly, which is at its greenest when the woods are bare, and in his other an axe, a huge and monstrous one, a cruel battle-axe to describe in words, if anyone could. The great head was more than a yard in length, the spike all forged of green steel and of gold, the blade brightly burnished and with a broad edge as well prepared for cutting as a sharpened razor. The grim figure gripped it by the handle, a stout staff which was wound round with iron to the end of the stave, and engraved all over with beautiful designs in green; around it lapped a thong, which was fastened at the head and then caught up many times along the shaft, with many fine tassels fastened to it by studs richly ornamented in the same bright green. The man came forward and entered the hall, making for the high table, regardless of danger; he greeted no one, but looked high over their heads. When at last he spoke, he said, 'Where is the ruler of this company? I would very much like to set eyes on that man and have speech with him.' He

To knyȝteȝ he kest his yȝe,
And reled hym vp and doun;
He stemmed and con studie
Quo walt þer most renoun.

Ther watȝ lokyng on lenþe, þe lude to beholde,
For vch mon had meruayle quat hit mene myȝt
Þat a haþel and a horse myȝt such a hwe lach
As growe grene as þe gres and grener hit semed,
Þen grene aumayl on golde glowande bryȝter.
Al studied þat þer stod, and stalked hym nerre
Wyth al þe wonder of þe worlde what he worch schulde.
For fele sellyeȝ had þay sen, bot such neuer are;
Forþi for fantoum and fayryȝe þe folk þere hit demed.
Þerfore to answare watȝ arȝe mony aþel freke,
And al stouned at his steuen and stonstil seten
In a swoghe sylence þurȝ þe sale riche.
As al were slypped vpon slepe so slaked hor loteȝ
in hyȝe—
I deme hit not al for doute,
Bot sum for cortaysye;
Bot let hym þat al schulde loute
Cast vnto þat wyȝe.

Þenn Arþour bifore þe hiȝ dece þat auenture byholdeȝ,
And rekenly hym reuerenced, for rad was he neuer,
And sayde, 'Wyȝe, welcum iwys to þis place.
Þe hede of þis ostel Arthour I hat.
Liȝt luflych adoun and lenge, I þe praye,
And quat-so þy wylle is we schal wyt after.'
'Nay, as help me,' quoþ þe haþel, 'he þat on hyȝe syttes,
To wone any quyle in þis won, hit watȝ not myn ernde.
Bot for þe los of þe, lede, is lyft vp so hyȝe,
And þy burȝ and þy burnes best ar holden,
Stifest vnder stel-gere on stedes to ryde,
Þe wyȝtest and þe worþyest of þe worldes kynde,
Preue for to play wyth in oþer pure laykeȝ,
And here is kydde cortaysye, as I haf herd carp—
And þat hatȝ wayned me hider, iwyis, at þis tyme.
Ȝe may be seker bi þis braunch þat I bere here

cast his gaze upon the knights, turning his eyes here and there; he paused, and carefully considered who there commanded most respect.

For a long moment they stared back, gazing at him, for everyone wondered what it could mean that a man and a horse should take on such a colour as to grow green as the grass and, it seemed, greener, glowing more brightly than green enamel over gold. All those in attendance there watched him intently, and cautiously walked closer to him with the greatest curiosity as to what he would do. For they had seen many marvels, but never such a one before; and so the people present thought it illusion and enchantment. For that reason many a noble knight was afraid to reply, and all were stunned by his words and sat stock-still in a dead silence throughout the royal hall. It was as if all had fallen asleep, so suddenly were their voices stilled—not altogether, I think, due to fear, but partly out of courtesy; but they left it to him to whom all should defer to speak to the man.

Then Arthur, gazing at that apparition before the high table, saluted him courteously, for he was not at all afraid, and said, 'Sir, you are truly welcome to this place. I am the head of this house and am called Arthur. Be so good as to dismount and stay with us, I beg you, and whatever your pleasure is we shall learn it later.' 'No,' said the man, 'so help me He who dwells on high, it was not my intent to stay any time in this place. But because your renown, my lord, is so loudly extolled, and your castle and your men are held to be the best, the strongest of mounted men-at-arms, the bravest and the best of human kind, valiant to contend with in various noble sports, and here chivalric courtesy is displayed, as I have heard tell—and that, indeed, is what has brought me here at this season. You may be assured by this branch that I carry

Þat I passe as in pes, and no plyȝt seche.
For had I founded in fere, in feȝtyng wyse,
I haue a hauberghe at home and a helme boþe,
A schelde and a scharp spere, schinande bryȝt,
Ande oþer weppenes to welde, I wene wel, als;
Bot for I wolde no were, my wedeȝ ar softer.
Bot if þou be so bold as alle burneȝ tellen,
Þou wyl grant me godly þe gomen þat I ask
        bi ryȝt.'
    Arthour con onsware,
    And sayd, 'Sir cortays knyȝt,
    If þou craue batayl bare,
    Here fayleȝ þou not to fyȝt.'

'Nay, frayst I no fyȝt, in fayth I þe telle.
Hit arn aboute on þis bench bot berdleȝ chylder;
If I were hasped in armes on a heȝe stede,
Here is no mon me to mach, for myȝteȝ so wayke.
Forþy I craue in þis court a Crystemas gomen,
For hit is Ȝol and Nwe Ȝer, and here ar ȝep mony.
If any so hardy in þis hous holdeȝ hymseluen,
Be so bolde in his blod, brayn in hys hede,
Þat dar stifly strike a strok for an oþer,
I schal gif hym of my gyft þys giserne ryche,
Þis ax, þat is heué innogh, to hondele as hym lykes,
And I schal bide þe fyrst bur as bare as I sitte.
If any freke be so felle to fonde þat I telle,
Lepe lyȝtly me to, and lach þis weppen;
I quit-clayme hit for euer, kepe hit as his auen,
And I schal stonde hym a strok, stif on þis flet,
Elleȝ þou wyl diȝt me þe dom to dele hym an oþer
        barlay;
    And ȝet gif hym respite
    A twelmonyth and a day.
    Now hyȝe, and let se tite
    Dar any herinne oȝt say.'

If he hem stowned vpon fyrst, stiller were þanne
Alle þe heredmen in halle, þe hyȝ and þe loȝe.
Þe renk on his rouncé hym ruched in his sadel,

here that I come in peace, and seek no contention. For had I come in force, in warlike fashion, I have a hauberk at home and a helmet as well, a shield and a sharp spear, shining bright, and other weapons too at my disposal, no doubt of that; but since I wish no strife, my dress is less warlike. But if you are as valiant as all men say, you will graciously grant me the sport that I ask for as my right.' Arthur answered, saying, 'Sir, courteous knight, if you are asking for single combat, here you will not fail to get a fight.'

'No, I seek no fight, I tell you honestly. There are none but beardless boys on these benches round about; if I were buckled in my armour on a tall steed, there is no man here to match me, so feeble are their powers. And so I ask in this court for a Christmas game, since it is Yuletide and New Year, and there are many brisk youths here. If anyone in this household considers himself so bold, and is so hot-blooded, so rash-headed, that he dare fearlessly strike one stroke in exchange for another, I shall give him as a gift from me this splendid halberd, this axe which is extremely heavy, to use as he pleases, and I shall undergo the first blow as unarmed as I sit here. If any man is so bold as to try what I suggest, let him quickly come to me, and take this weapon; I surrender it for ever, let him keep it as his own. And I shall stand and take a blow from him, unflinching, on this spot, provided you will award me the right to deal him another when I claim it; and yet I will give him respite for a year and a day. Quickly now, and let us see at once if anyone here dare say anything.'

If he had stunned them at first, now they were even more abashed, all the retainers in the hall, the great and the lowly. The man on horseback twisted himself in his saddle, his fiery eyes fiercely turning here and

And runischly his rede yȝen he reled aboute,
Bende his bresed broȝeȝ, blycande grene,
Wayued his berde for to wayte quo-so wolde ryse.
When non wolde kepe hym with carp he coȝed ful hyȝe,
Ande rimed hym ful richely, and ryȝt hym to speke:
'What, is þis Arþures hous,' quoþ þe haþel þenne,
'Þat al þe rous rennes of þurȝ ryalmes so mony?
Where is now your sourquydrye and your conquestes,
Your gryndellayk and your greme and your grete wordes?
Now is þe reuel and þe renoun of þe Rounde Table
Ouerwalt wyth a worde of on wyȝes speche,
For al dares for drede withoute dynt schewed!'
Wyth þis he laȝes so loude þat þe lorde greued;
Þe blod schot for scham into his schyre face
          and lere;
     He wex as wroth as wynde,
     So did alle þat þer were.
     Þe kyng as kene bi kynde
     Þen stod þat stif mon nere,

Ande sayde, 'Haþel, by heuen þyn askyng is nys,
And as þou foly hatȝ frayst, fynde þe behoues.
I know no gome þat is gast of þy grete wordes.
Gif me now þy geserne, vpon Godeȝ halue,
And I schal bayþen þy bone þat þou boden habbes.'
Lyȝtly lepeȝ he hym to, and laȝt at his honde.
Þen feersly þat oþer freke vpon fote lyȝtis.
Now hatȝ Arthure his axe, and þe halme grypeȝ,
And sturnely stureȝ hit aboute, þat stryke wyth hit þoȝt.
Þe stif mon hym bifore stod vpon hyȝt,
Herre þen ani in þe hous by þe hede and more.
Wyth sturne schere þer he stod, he stroked his berde,
And wyth a countenaunce dryȝe he droȝ doun his cote,
No more mate ne dismayd for hys mayn dinteȝ,
Þen any burne vpon bench hade broȝt hym to drynk
          of wyne.
     Gawan, þat sate bi þe quene,
     To þe kyng he can enclyne:
     'I beseche now with saȝeȝ sene
     Þis melly mot be myne.

there, his bristling brows knitted, gleaming green, his beard sweeping from side to side, to see who would rise. When no one would speak with him, he cleared his throat very loudly, and drew himself up magnificently, and proceeded to speak: 'What! is this Arthur's house,' said the man then, 'about which all the talk runs through so many realms? Where now are your pride and your triumphs, your ferocity and your anger, and your bragging words? Now the revelry and the renown of the Round Table have been overthrown by a single word from one man's mouth, for all of you are cowering with fear without a blow being offered!' With this he laughed so loudly that the prince was offended; for very shame the blood rushed into his handsome face and cheek; he grew as furious as the wind, as did all who were there. The king, being valiant by nature, instantly stood by that bold man's side,

and said, 'By heaven! sir, your request is foolish, and as you have asked for a foolish thing, you deserve to have it. I know no man who is afraid of your threats. Give me your axe at once, for God's sake, and I will grant you the boon that you have requested.' Swiftly he steps up to him and seizes his hand. Then the other man proudly dismounts. Now Arthur takes his axe, grips the handle, and grimly swings it around, as if intending to strike. The man, unmoved, stood towering before him, taller than anyone in the house by a head and more. With a grim face he stood there stroking his beard, and with a countenance unmoved he drew down his tunic, no more daunted or dismayed by Arthur's mighty strokes than if someone at the table had brought him some wine to drink. Gawain, who was seated beside the queen, bowed to the king: 'I beg you now in plain words that this contest may be mine.

'Wolde ȝe, worþilych lorde,' quoþ Wawan to þe kyng,
'Bid me boȝe fro þis benche and stonde by yow þere,
Þat I wythoute vylanye myȝt voyde þis table,
And þat my legge lady lyked not ille,
I wolde com to your counseyl bifore your cort ryche.
For me þink hit not semly, as hit is soþ knawen,
Þer such an askyng is heuened so hyȝe in your sale,
Þaȝ ȝe ȝourself be talenttyf, to take hit to yourseluen,
Whil mony so bolde yow aboute vpon bench sytten,
Þat vnder heuen, I hope, non haȝerer of wylle,
Ne better bodyes on bent þer baret is rered.
I am þe wakkest, I wot, and of wyt feblest,
And lest lur of my lyf, quo laytes þe soþe.
Bot for as much as ȝe ar myn em I am only to prayse;
No bounté bot your blod I in my bodé knowe.
And syþen þis note is so nys þat noȝt hit yow falles,
And I haue frayned hit at yow fyrst, foldeȝ hit to me;
And if I carp not comlyly, let alle þis cort rych
        bout blame.'
    Ryche togeder con roun,
    And syþen þay redden alle same
    To ryd þe kyng wyth croun,
    And gif Gawan þe game.

Þen comaunded þe kyng þe knyȝt for to ryse;
And he ful radly vp ros, and ruchched hym fayre,
Kneled doun bifore þe kyng, and cacheȝ þat weppen.
And he luflyly hit hym laft, and lyfte vp his honde,
And gef hym Goddeȝ blessyng, and gladly hym biddes
Þat his hert and his honde schulde hardi be boþe.
'Kepe þe, cosyn,' quoþ þe kyng, 'þat þou on kyrf sette,
And if þou redeȝ hym ryȝt, redly I trowe
Þat þou schal byden þe bur þat he schal bede after.'
Gawan gotȝ to þe gome with giserne in honde,
And he baldly hym bydeȝ, he bayst neuer þe helder.
Þen carppeȝ to Sir Gawan þe knyȝt in þe grene:
'Refourme we oure forwardes, er we fyrre passe.
Fyrst I eþe þe, haþel, how þat þou hattes,
Þat þou me telle truly, as I tryst may.'
'In god fayth,' quoþ þe goode knyȝt, 'Gawan I hatte,

'If you, my honoured lord,' said Gawain to the king, 'would command me to quit this seat and stand by you there, so that without discourtesy I might leave this table, and provided my sovereign lady would not be displeased, I would come to consult with you in the presence of your noble court. For it seems to me not fitting, as is manifestly true, when a challenge like this is voiced so arrogantly in your hall, that you should take it upon yourself, though you personally may be eager to, while on the benches around you sit many men so bold that none on this earth, I believe, are readier in temper, nor better men on a battlefield when strife is stirred up. I am the weakest, I know, and the most deficient in understanding, and my life would be the smallest loss, if the truth be known. I am only to be esteemed in as much as you are my uncle; I acknowledge no virtue in myself except your blood. And since this business is so foolish that it is unfitting for you, and I have asked it of you first, it properly belongs to me; and whether or not I speak fittingly, let this whole court decide without offence.' The nobles whispered together, and then they one and all advised that the reigning king should be exempted and the contest given to Gawain.

Then the king commanded the knight to rise from table; and he promptly arose, came forward courteously, knelt down before the king and took the weapon. And he graciously surrendered it and, lifting up his hand, gave him God's blessing, and cheerfully urged him that his heart and his hand should both be resolute. 'Take care, cousin,' said the king, 'that you give one stroke, and if you deal with him properly, I fully believe that you will survive any blow he shall offer you afterwards.' Gawain goes towards the man with axe in hand, and he boldly awaits him, not a whit more dismayed. Then the knight in green speaks to Sir Gawain: 'Let us restate the terms of our agreement, before we go any further. First I beg you, knight, that you will tell me truly what you are called, that I can have faith in you.' 'Truly,' said the good knight, 'I am called Gawain,

Þat bede þe þis buffet, quat-so bifalleȝ after,
And at þis tyme twelmonyth take at þe anoþer
Wyth what weppen so þou wylt, and wyth no wyȝ elleȝ
        on lyue.'
    Þat oþer onswareȝ agayn:
    'Sir Gawan, so mot I þryue,
    As I am ferly fayn
    Þis dint þat þou schal dryue.

'Bigog,' quoþ þe grene knyȝt, 'Sir Gawan, me lykes
Þat I schal fange at þy fust þat I haf frayst here.
And þou hatȝ redily rehersed, bi resoun ful trwe,
Clanly al þe couenaunt þat I þe kynge asked,
Saf þat þou schal siker me, segge, bi þi trawþe,
Þat þou schal seche me þiself, where-so þou hopes
I may be funde vpon folde, and foch þe such wages
As þou deles me to-day bifore þis douþe ryche.'
'Where schulde I wale þe,' quoþ Gauan, 'where is þy place?
I wot neuer where þou wonyes, bi hym þat me wroȝt,
Ne I know not þe, knyȝt, þy cort ne þi name.
Bot teche me truly þerto, and telle me howe þou hattes,
And I schal ware alle my wyt to wynne me þeder,
And þat I swere þe for soþe, and by my seker traweþ.'
'Þat is innogh in Nwe Ȝer; hit nedes no more,'
Quoþ þe gome in þe grene to Gawan þe hende.
'Ȝif I þe telle trwly, quen I þe tape haue
And þou me smoþely hatȝ smyten, smartly I þe teche
Of my hous and my home and myn owen nome,
Þen may þou frayst my fare and forwardeȝ holde;
And if I spende no speche, þenne spedeȝ þou þe better,
For þou may leng in þy londe and layt no fyrre.
        Bot slokes!
    Ta now þy grymme tole to þe,
    And let se how þou cnokeȝ.'
    'Gladly, sir, for soþe,'
    Quoþ Gawan; his ax he strokes.

The grene knyȝt vpon grounde grayþely hym dresses:
A littel lut with þe hede, þe lere he discouereȝ;
His longe louelych lokkeȝ he layd ouer his croun,

I who offer you this blow, come what may in consequence, and will a year from now accept another from you with whatever weapon you wish, and from no living soul other than you.' The other replied: 'Sir Gawain, upon my life, I am extremely glad that you are to strike this blow.

'By God, Sir Gawain,' said the Green Knight, 'it pleases me that I shall receive from your hand what I have asked for here. And you have correctly repeated, in exact terms, without omission, the whole compact which I requested of the king, save that you shall give me your word, sir, that you will seek me on your own, wherever you think I may be found on this earth, and yourself receive such payment as you mete out to me today before this noble assembly.' 'Where should I seek you,' said Gawain, 'where is your dwelling-place? I know nothing about where you live, by Him who made me, nor do I know you, sir, the court from which you come, or your name. But direct me to it clearly, and tell me what you are called, and I shall employ all my wits to get myself there, and this I swear to you truly on my plighted troth.' 'That is sufficient at New Year; no more is needed,' said the man in green to the courteous Gawain. 'If I tell you correctly when I have had the tap and you have deftly struck me, if I promptly inform you about my house and my home and my own name, then you may enquire after my welfare and keep the agreement; and if I say nothing, then you will be all the better off, for you can stay in your own country and concern yourself no further. But enough! Now take your grim weapon in hand and let us see how you strike.' 'Gladly, sir, indeed,' said Gawain, stroking his axe.

The Green Knight at once took up his stance; bending his head a little, he exposed the flesh; throwing his beautiful long locks forward over

Let þe naked nec to þe note schewe.
Gauan gripped to his ax, and gederes hit on hyȝt,
Þe kay fot on þe folde he before sette,
Let hit doun lyȝtly lyȝt on þe naked,
Þat þe scharp of þe schalk schyndered þe bones,
And schrank þurȝ þe schyire grece, and schade hit in twynne,
Þat þe bit of þe broun stel bot on þe grounde.
Þe fayre hede fro þe halce hit to þe erþe,
Þat fele hit foyned wyth her fete, þere hit forth roled;
Þe blod brayd fro þe body, þat blykked on þe grene.
And nawþer faltered ne fel þe freke neuer þe helder,
Bot styþly he start forth vpon styf schonkes,
And runyschly he raȝt out, þere as renkkeȝ stoden,
Laȝt to his lufly hed, and lyft hit vp sone;
And syþen boȝeȝ to his blonk, þe brydel he cachcheȝ,
Steppeȝ into stelbawe and strydeȝ alofte,
And his hede by þe here in his honde haldeȝ;
And as sadly þe segge hym in his sadel sette
As non vnhap had hym ayled, þaȝ hedleȝ nowe
in stedde.
He brayde his bluk aboute,
Þat vgly bodi þat bledde;
Moni on of hym had doute,
Bi þat his resounȝ were redde.

For þe hede in his honde he haldeȝ vp euen,
Toward þe derrest on þe dece he dresseȝ þe face,
And hit lyfte vp þe yȝe-lyddeȝ and loked ful brode,
And meled þus much with his muthe, as ȝe may now here:
'Loke, Gawan, þou be grayþe to go as þou hetteȝ,
And layte as lelly til þou me, lude, fynde,
As þou hatȝ hette in þis halle, herande þise knyȝtes.
To þe grene chapel þou chose, I charge þe, to fotte
Such a dunt as þou hatȝ dalt—disserued þou habbeȝ,
To be ȝederly ȝolden on Nw Ȝeres morn.
Þe knyȝt of þe grene chapel men knowen me mony;
Forþi me for to fynde if þou fraysteȝ, fayleȝ þou neuer.
Þerfore com, oþer recreaunt be calde þe behoues.'
With a runisch rout þe rayneȝ he torneȝ,
Halled out at þe hal dor, his hed in his hande,

his head, he let the naked neck appear in readiness. Gawain took a grip on his axe, and, lifting it up high, with the left foot advanced, brought it down deftly on the naked flesh, so that the man's own sharp weapon cleaved his bones, and sank through the fair flesh, severing it in two, so that the bright steel blade bit into the ground. The handsome head fell from the neck to the floor, and many spurned it with their feet as it rolled towards them; the blood spurted from the body and glistened on the green garments. And yet the man neither staggered at all nor fell as a result, but undismayed he sprang forward upon firm legs, and fiercely he reached out amongst the people's feet, seized his handsome head, and quickly lifted it up; and then, turning to his horse, caught the bridle, stepped into the stirrup and vaulted up, holding his head by the hair in his hand; and the knight seated himself in his saddle as calmly as if he had suffered no mishap, though he sat there headless now. He twisted his trunk around, that gruesome bleeding corpse; many were in fear of him by the time he had had his say.

For he actually held up the head in his hand, turning the face toward the greatest nobles on the dais, and it lifted up its eyelids and stared wide-eyed, and its mouth spoke, as you may now hear, to this effect: 'See to it, Gawain, that you are ready to go as you promised, and search until you find me, sir, as faithfully as you have sworn in this hall, in the hearing of these knights. Make your way to the Green Chapel, I charge you, to receive such a knock as you have given—you have well deserved to be promptly repaid on New Year's morning. Many men know me, the Knight of the Green Chapel; and so, if you seek to find me, you will not fail. Come, therefore, or you are bound to be called a coward.' With a violent jerk he pulled the reins round and, his head in his hand, dashed out at the door of the hall, so that the sparks flew

Þat þe fyr of þe flynt flaȝe fro fole houes.
To quat kyth he becom knwe non þere,
Neuer more þen þay wyste fram queþen he watȝ wonnen.
What þenne?
Þe kyng and Gawen þare
At þat grene þay laȝe and grenne;
Ȝet breued watȝ hit ful bare
A meruayl among þo menne.

Þaȝ Arþer þe hende kyng at hert hade wonder,
He let no semblaunt be sene, bot sayde ful hyȝe
To þe comlych quene wyth cortays speche,
'Dere dame, to-day demay yow neuer;
Wel bycommes such craft vpon Cristmasse,
Laykyng of enterludeȝ, to laȝe and to syng,
Among þise kynde caroles of knyȝteȝ and ladyeȝ.
Neuer þe lece to my mete I may me wel dres,
For I haf sen a selly, I may not forsake.'
He glent vpon Sir Gawen, and gaynly he sayde,
'Now sir, heng vp þyn ax, þat hatȝ innogh hewen.'
And hit watȝ don abof þe dece on doser to henge,
Þer alle men for meruayl myȝt on hit loke,
And bi trwe tytel þerof to telle þe wonder.
Þenne þay boȝed to a borde þise burnes togeder,
Þe kyng and þe gode knyȝt, and kene men hem serued
Of alle dayntyeȝ double, as derrest myȝt falle.
Wyth alle maner of mete and mynstralcie boþe,
Wyth wele walt þay þat day, til worþed an ende
in londe.
Now þenk wel, Sir Gawan,
For woþe þat þou ne wonde
Þis auenture for to frayn
Þat þou hatȝ tan on honde.

II

This hanselle hatȝ Arthur of auenturus on fyrst
In ȝonge ȝer, for he ȝerned ȝelpyng to here.
Thaȝ hym wordeȝ were wane when þay to sete wenten,

from the stones at his horse's hooves. To what land he went none there knew, any more than they knew where he had come from. What then? The king and Gawain then laughed at the green man, smiling broadly; yet amongst the people there it was openly spoken of as a marvel.

Though the noble king Arthur was amazed at heart, he let no sign appear, but said aloud, addressing the fair queen in courteous words, 'Dear lady, let nothing perturb you today; such doings are very proper at Christmas time, playing of interludes, laughing and singing, among the seasonal pastimes of knights and ladies. None the less I can properly betake myself to my meal, for I have seen a marvel, I cannot deny it.' He looked at Sir Gawain and said aptly, 'Now, sir, hang up your axe, which has hewn enough'; and it was placed above the dais to hang against the wall-tapestry, where everyone could look at it as a marvellous thing, and with its manifest authority relate the strange event. Then both men sat down to table together, the king and the good knight, and were promptly served a double portion of every delicacy, as the most noble should rightly be. With all sorts of food and all kinds of music and song as well, they passed the day pleasantly, till it drew to an end on earth. Now take good heed, Sir Gawain, that you do not shrink because of danger from pursuing this adventure which you have undertaken.

II

This foretaste of adventures Arthur received at the beginning of the new year, for he ever longed to hear of bold deeds. Though matter for discussion was lacking when they went to table, now they are fully

Now ar þay stoken of sturne werk, stafful her hond.
Gawan watȝ glad to begynne þose gomneȝ in halle,
Bot þaȝ þe ende be heuy haf ȝe no wonder;
For þaȝ men ben mery in mynde quen þay han mayn drynk,
A ȝere ȝernes ful ȝerne, and ȝeldeȝ neuer lyke,
Þe forme to þe fynisment foldeȝ ful selden.
Forþi þis Ȝol ouerȝede, and þe ȝere after,
And vche sesoun serlepes sued after oþer:
After Crystenmasse com þe crabbed lentoun,
Þat fraysteȝ flesch wyth þe fysche and fode more symple;
Bot þenne þe weder of þe worlde wyth wynter hit þrepeȝ,
Colde clengeȝ adoun, cloudeȝ vplyften,
Schyre schedeȝ þe rayn in schowereȝ ful warme,
Falleȝ vpon fayre flat, flowreȝ þere schewen,
Boþe groundeȝ and þe greueȝ grene ar her wedeȝ,
Bryddeȝ busken to bylde, and bremlych syngen
For solace of þe softe somer þat sues þerafter
            bi bonk;
      And blossumeȝ bolne to blowe
      Bi raweȝ rych and ronk,
      Þen noteȝ noble innoȝe
      Ar herde in wod so wlonk.

After þe sesoun of somer wyth þe soft wyndeȝ,
Quen Ȝeferus syfleȝ hymself on sedeȝ and erbeȝ,
Wela wynne is þe wort þat waxes þeroute,
When þe donkande dewe dropeȝ of þe leueȝ,
To bide a blysful blusch of þe bryȝt sunne.
Bot þen hyȝes heruest, and hardenes hym sone,
Warneȝ hym for þe wynter to wax ful rype;
He dryues wyth droȝt þe dust for to ryse,
Fro þe face of þe folde to flyȝe ful hyȝe;
Wroþe wynde of þe welkyn wrasteleȝ with þe sunne,
Þe leueȝ lancen fro þe lynde and lyȝten on þe grounde,
And al grayes þe gres þat grene watȝ ere;
Þenne al rypeȝ and roteȝ þat ros vpon fyrst,
And þus ȝirneȝ þe ȝere in ȝisterdayeȝ mony,
And wynter wyndeȝ aȝayn, as þe worlde askeȝ,
            no fage,

531 fage: MS sage

occupied with serious business, their hands are cram-full. Gawain was happy to begin those sports in the hall, but do not be surprised if the end should be sad; for though men may be light-hearted when they have drunk strong drink, a year passes very quickly, and never brings back like circumstances, the beginning is very seldom like the end. And so this Yuletide passed by, and the year after it, and each season in turn followed after the other: after Christmas there came meagre Lent, which tries the flesh with its fish and plainer fare; but then the weather everywhere contends against winter, cold shrinks down into the earth, the clouds lift, bright falls the rain in warm showers, falls upon the fair plain where flowers appear, the fields and groves alike are clothed in green, birds make haste to build, gaily singing their delight in the mild summer which follows next upon the hillsides; and blossoms swell into bloom along hedgerows richly overgrown, while many glorious songs are heard in the lovely wood.

With the coming of the summer season with its gentle breezes, when the West Wind breathes himself into seeds and grasses, there springs from them the most lovely growth, when the moistening dew drips from the leaves, and it enjoys a pleasant glance from the bright sun. But then autumn hastens on, and matures it quickly, warning it to grow fully ripe in readiness for winter; by drought he drives the dust to rise, to fly far, far up from the face of the earth; in the heavens above a wild wind wrestles with the sun, the leaves fly from the linden tree and light upon the ground, and the grass which once was green becomes quite grey; then all that sprang up in the beginning ripens and decays, and so the year runs by in many passing days, and winter returns again, as is, to be sure, the way of the world, until the Michaelmas moon was come

Til Meȝelmas mone
Watȝ cumen wyth wynter wage.
Þen þenkkeȝ Gawan ful sone
Of his anious uyage.

Ȝet quyl Al-hal-day with Arþer he lenges;
And he made a fare on þat fest for þe frekeȝ sake,
With much reuel and ryche of þe Rounde Table.
Knyȝteȝ ful cortays and comlych ladies
Al for luf of þat lede in longynge þay were,
Bot neuer þe lece ne þe later þay neuened bot merþe:
Mony ioyleȝ for þat ientyle iapeȝ þer maden.
For aftter mete with mournyng he meleȝ to his eme,
And spekeȝ of his passage, and pertly he sayde,
'Now, lege lorde of my lyf, leue I yow ask.
Ȝe knowe þe cost of þis cace, kepe I no more
To telle yow teneȝ þerof, neuer bot trifel;
Bot I am boun to þe bur barely to-morne,
To sech þe gome of þe grene, as God wyl me wysse.'
Þenne þe best of þe burȝ boȝed togeder,
Aywan, and Errik, and oþer ful mony,
Sir Doddinaual de Sauage, þe duk of Clarence,
Launcelot, and Lyonel, and Lucan þe gode,
Sir Boos, and Sir Byduer, big men boþe,
And mony oþer menskful, with Mador de la Port.
Alle þis compayny of court com þe kyng nerre
For to counseyl þe knyȝt, with care at her hert.
Þere watȝ much derne doel driuen in þe sale
Þat so worthé as Wawan schulde wende on þat ernde,
To dryȝe a delful dynt, and dele no more
wyth bronde.
Þe knyȝt mad ay god chere,
And sayde, 'Quat schuld I wonde?
Of destinés derf and dere
What may mon do bot fonde?'

He dowelleȝ þer al þat day, and dresseȝ on þe morn,
Askeȝ erly hys armeȝ, and alle were þay broȝt.
Fyrst a tulé tapit tyȝt ouer þe flet,
And miche watȝ þe gyld gere þat glent þeralofte.

with forewarning of winter. Then Gawain all at once recalls his difficult quest.

Yet until All Saints' Day he remained with Arthur; and he made a feast on that festival for the knight's sake, with much splendid revelry of the Round Table. Courteous knights and lovely ladies were in distress, all for love of that man, but yet they were none the less ready to speak only of pleasant things: many there made jests who were sad at heart for that gentle knight. For after dinner he spoke with concern to his uncle, and talked of his joumey, and said frankly, 'Now, sovereign lord of my life, I ask your leave to go. You know the nature of this affair, and I do not care to speak to you further about the difficulties involved, it would only be a waste of breath; but I am to set out for the return blow tomorrow without fail, to seek the Green Knight, as God shall guide me.' Then the best knights in the castle came together, Ywain, and Erec, and very many others, Sir Dodinel de Savage, the Duke of Clarence, Lancelot, and Lionel, and the good Sir Lucan, Sir Bors, and Sir Bedivere, both eminent men, and many other nobles, including Mador de la Port. All this courtly company gathered round the king to advise the knight, with grief in their hearts. Much secret sorrow was felt in the hall that one so distinguished as Gawain should have to go on that mission, to suffer a grievous blow, and strike none in return with his sword. The knight remained cheerful throughout, and said, 'What should I shrink from? What can one do but plumb to the depths what Fate holds in store, painful and pleasant alike?'

He remained there all that day, and next day prepared himself, asked early for his arms, and they were all brought. First a silken carpet was spread over the floor, on which much gilded armour gleamed. The

Þe stif mon steppeȝ þeron, and þe stel hondeleȝ,
Dubbed in a dublet of a dere tars,
And syþen a crafty capados, closed aloft,
Þat wyth a bryȝt blaunner was bounden withinne.
Þenne set þay þe sabatounȝ vpon þe segge foteȝ,
His legeȝ lapped in stel with luflych greueȝ,
With polayneȝ piched þerto, policed ful clene,
Aboute his kneȝ knaged wyth knoteȝ of golde;
Queme quyssewes þen, þat coyntlych closed
His thik þrawen þyȝeȝ, with þwonges to tachched;
And syþen þe brawden bryné of bryȝt stel ryngeȝ
Vmbeweued þat wyȝ, vpon wlonk stuffe,
And wel bornyst brace vpon his boþe armes,
With gode cowters and gay, and gloueȝ of plate,
And alle þe godlych gere þat hym gayn schulde
        þat tyde;
    Wyth ryche cote-armure,
    His gold sporeȝ spend with pryde,
    Gurde wyth a bront ful sure
    With silk sayn vmbe his syde.

When he watȝ hasped in armes, his harnays watȝ ryche:
Þe lest lachet oþer loupe lemed of golde.
So harnayst as he watȝ he herkneȝ his masse,
Offred and honoured at þe heȝe auter.
Syþen he comeȝ to þe kyng and to his cort-fereȝ,
Lacheȝ lufly his leue at lordeȝ and ladyeȝ,
And þay hym kyst and conueyed, bikende hym to Kryst.
Bi þat watȝ Gryngolet grayth, and gurde with a sadel
Þat glemed ful gayly with mony golde frenges,
Ayquere naylet ful nwe, for þat note ryched;
Þe brydel barred aboute, with bryȝt golde bounden;
Þe apparayl of þe payttrure and of þe proude skyrteȝ,
Þe cropore and þe couertor, acorded wyth þe arsouneȝ;
And al watȝ rayled on red ryche golde nayleȝ,
Þat al glytered and glent as glem of þe sunne.
Þenne hentes he þe helme, and hastily hit kysses,
Þat watȝ stapled stifly, and stoffed wythinne.
Hit watȝ hyȝe on his hede, hasped bihynde,
Wyth a lyȝtly vrysoun ouer þe auentayle,

bold man stepped on to it, and handled the arms, clad in a tunic of costly Tharsian silk, and over that a hooded cape, skilfully made, fastened at the neck, and trimmed inside with a pure white fur. Then they put the steel shoes upon the knight's feet, his legs were lapped in steel by handsome greaves, to which were attached knee-pieces, very brightly polished, fastened about his knees with ties of gold; next fine thigh-pieces, which elegantly encased his stout muscular thighs, and were fastened with thongs; and then the linked corslet of bright steel rings enveloped the knight, covering his splendid clothing, and well burnished arm-pieces on his two arms, with good, bright elbow-pieces, and gauntlets of plate, and all the fine equipment which would be of use to him on that occasion; together with a costly surcoat, his gold spurs fastened on with ceremony, a trusty sword girt about his waist by a silken girdle.

When he was encased in armour, his gear was splendid: the smallest lace or loop shone with gold. Armed thus as he was he heard his Mass, offered and celebrated at the high altar. Then he came to the king and to his companions at court, courteously took his leave of the lords and ladies, and they kissed him and escorted him out, commending him to Christ. By that time Gryngolet was ready, and girt with a saddle that shone gaily with many gold fringes, newly studded all over, specially prepared for that occasion; the bridle was ringed round, bound with bright gold; the decoration of the breast-trappings and of the magnificent saddle-flaps, the crupper and the horse-cloth, matched that of the saddle-bows; and everywhere, set upon a red ground, were splendid gold nails, which all glittered and glinted like rays of sunlight. Then he took up and quickly kissed the helmet, which was stapled strongly and padded inside. It sat high on his head, secured behind, with a band of fine silk above the chain-mail neck-guard, embroidered

Enbrawden and bounden wyth þe best gemmeȝ
On brode sylkyn borde, and bryddeȝ on semeȝ,
As papiayeȝ paynted peruyng bitwene,
Tortors and trulofeȝ entayled so þyk
As mony burde þeraboute had ben seuen wynter
    in toune.
  Þe cercle watȝ more o prys
  Þat vmbeclypped hys croun,
  Of diamaunteȝ a deuys,
  Þat boþe were bryȝt and broun.

Then þay schewed hym þe schelde, þat was of schyr gouleȝ
Wyth þe pentangel depaynt of pure golde hweȝ.
He braydeȝ hit by þe bauderyk, aboute þe hals kestes,
Þat bisemed þe segge semlyly fayre.
And quy þe pentangel apendeȝ to þat prynce noble
I am in tent yow to telle, þof tary hyt me schulde:
Hit is a syngne þat Salamon set sumquyle
In bytoknyng of trawþe, bi tytle þat hit habbeȝ,
For hit is a figure þat haldeȝ fyue poynteȝ,
And vche lyne vmbelappeȝ and loukeȝ in oþer,
And ayquere hit is endeleȝ; and Englych hit callen
Oueral, as I here, þe endeles knot.
Forþy hit acordeȝ to þis knyȝt and to his cler armeȝ;
For ay faythful in fyue and sere fyue syþeȝ,
Gawan watȝ for gode knawen, and as golde pured,
Voyded of vche vylany, wyth vertueȝ ennoured
    in mote.
  Forþy þe pentangel nwe
  He ber in schelde and cote,
  As tulk of tale most trwe
  And gentylest knyȝt of lote.

Fyrst he watȝ funden fautleȝ in his fyue wytteȝ,
And efte fayled neuer þe freke in his fyue fyngres,
And alle his afyaunce vpon folde watȝ in þe fyue woundeȝ
Þat Cryst kaȝt on þe croys, as þe crede telleȝ.
And quere-so-euer þys mon in melly watȝ stad,
His þro þoȝt watȝ in þat, þurȝ alle oþer þyngeȝ,
Þat alle his forsnes he fong at þe fyue joyeȝ

and set with the best gems on its broad silken hem, and along the seams, birds such as parrots depicted amongst periwinkle plants, turtle-doves and true-love flowers embroidered as closely as if many ladies at court had been engaged on it for seven years. The circlet which encompassed his brow was more precious still, composed of flawless diamonds which were both clear and clouded.

Then they displayed for him the shield, which was of bright gules with the pentangle picked out in the colour of pure gold. He seized the shield by the baldric and slung it about his neck; it suited the knight fittingly and well. And just why the pentangle is appropriate to that noble lord I am bent on telling you, even though it should delay me: it is a symbol that Solomon devised once upon a time as a token of fidelity, appropriately, for it is a figure which contains five points, and each line overlaps and interlocks with another, and it is unbroken anywhere; and all over England, so I hear, it is called the endless knot. And so it is appropriate to this knight and to his unblemished arms; because he was always trustworthy in five respects and fivefold in each, Gawain was known to be a good knight, and like refined gold, free from every imperfection, graced with chivalric virtues. For this reason he bore the pentangle newly depicted upon shield and surcoat, as being a man most true to his word and in bearing the noblest of knights.

first, he was proved faultless in his five senses, and secondly the knight was never at fault through his five fingers, and all his trust on this earth was in the five wounds which Christ received on the cross, as the Creed tells. And wherever this man was beset in battle, his steadfast thought was upon this, above all else—that he should draw all his

Þat þe hende heuen-quene had of hir chylde;
At þis cause þe knyȝt comlyche hade
In þe inore half of his schelde hir ymage depaynted,
Þat quen he blusched þerto his belde neuer payred.
Þe fyft fyue þat I finde þat þe frek vsed
Watȝ fraunchyse and felaȝschyp forbe al þyng,
His clannes and his cortaysye croked were neuer,
And pité, þat passeȝ alle poynteȝ, þyse pure fyue
Were harder happed on þat haþel þen on any oþer.
Now alle þese fyue syþeȝ, for soþe, were fetled on þis knyȝt,
And vchone halched in oþer, þat non ende hade,
And fyched vpon fyue poynteȝ þat fayld neuer,
Ne samned neuer in no syde, ne sundred nouþer,
Withouten ende at any noke I oquere fynde,
Whereeuer þe gomen bygan or glod to an ende.
Þerfore on his schene schelde schapen watȝ þe knot
Ryally wyth red golde vpon rede gowleȝ,
Þat is þe pure pentaungel wyth þe peple called
with lore.
Now grayþed is Gawan gay,
And laȝt his launce ryȝt þore,
And gef hem alle goud day—
He wende for euermore.

He sperred þe sted with þe spureȝ and sprong on his way,
So stif þat þe ston-fyr stroke out þerafter.
Al þat seȝ þat semly syked in hert,
And sayde soþly al same segges til oþer,
Carande for þat comly: 'Bi Kryst, hit is scaþe
Þat þou, leude, schal be lost, þat art of lyf noble!
To fynde hys fere vpon folde, in fayth, is not eþe.
Warloker to haf wroȝt had more wyt bene,
And haf dyȝt ȝonder dere a duk to haue worþed;
A lowande leder of ledeȝ in londe hym wel semeȝ,
And so had better haf ben þen britned to noȝt,
Hadet wyth an aluisch mon, for angardeȝ pryde.
Who knew euer any kyng such counsel to take
As knyȝteȝ in cauelaciounȝ on Crystmasse gomneȝ!'
Wel much watȝ þe warme water þat waltered of yȝen
When þat semly syre soȝt fro þo woneȝ
þad daye.

fortitude from the five joys which the gracious Queen of Heaven had in her child; for this reason the knight appropriately had her image depicted on the inner side of his shield, so that when he looked at it his courage never failed. The fifth group of five which I find the man displayed was generosity and love of his fellow men above all else, his purity and his courtesy were never at fault, and compassion, which surpasses all other qualities, these five virtues were more firmly attached to that man than to any other. Now all these five groups were, in truth, conjoined in this knight, each one linked to another, so that none had an end, established upon five points that were ever fixed, none coinciding anywhere nor separating either, and all without end at any place I can find anywhere, wherever the tracing process began or came to an end. Accordingly there was fashioned upon his bright shield, splendid in red gold upon the crimson gules, the device which is called by learned men the perfect pentangle. Now Gawain was finely arrayed, and there and then he took his lance and bade them all good day—for ever, as he thought.

He set spurs to the horse and sprang on his way, so vigorously that sparks were struck from the stones behind him. All who saw that splendid sight sighed in their hearts, and all the people alike said quietly to each other, grieving for that fair knight: 'By Christ, it is a pity that you, sir, who are so noble in your life, are to perish! To find his equal on this earth, truly, is not easy. It would have been wiser to have acted with more caution, and to have appointed that noble man to be a duke; to be a brilliant leader of men in this land would well befit him, and he had better have been so than be destroyed utterly, beheaded by an elvish man because of overweening pride. Who ever knew any king to take such counsel as knights give in quibbling over Christmas games!' Much warm water gushed from their eyes when that fair knight went

He made non abode,
Bot wyȝtly went hys way;
Mony wylsum way he rode,
Þe bok as I herde say.

Now rideȝ þis renk þurȝ þe ryalme of Logres,
Sir Gauan, on Godeȝ halue, þaȝ hym no gomen þoȝt.
Oft leudleȝ alone he lengeȝ on nyȝteȝ
Þer he fonde noȝt hym byfore þe fare þat he lyked.
Hade he no fere bot his fole bi frytheȝ and douneȝ,
Ne no gome bot God bi gate wyth to karp,
Til þat he neȝed ful neghe into þe Norþe Waleȝ.
Alle þe iles of Anglesay on lyft half he haldeȝ,
And fareȝ ouer þe fordeȝ by þe forlondeȝ,
Ouer at þe Holy Hede, til he hade eft bonk
In þe wyldrenesse of Wyrale; wonde þer bot lyte
Þat auþer God oþer gome wyth goud hert louied.
And ay he frayned, as he ferde, at frekeȝ þat he met,
If þay hade herde any karp of a knyȝt grene,
In any grounde þeraboute, of þe grene chapel;
And al nykked hym wyth nay, þat neuer in her lyue
Þay seȝe neuer no segge þat watȝ of suche hweȝ
of grene.
Þe knyȝt tok gates straunge
In mony a bonk vnbene;
His cher ful oft con chaunge,
Þat chapel er he myȝt sene.

Mony klyf he ouerclambe in contrayeȝ straunge;
Fer floten fro his frendeȝ fremedly he rydeȝ.
At vche warþe oþer water þer þe wyȝe passed
He fonde a foo hym byfore, bot ferly hit were,
And þat so foule and so felle þat feȝt hym byhode.
So mony meruayl bi mount þer þe mon fyndeȝ,
Hit were to tore for to telle of þe tenþe dole.
Sumwhyle wyth wormeȝ he werreȝ, and with wolues als,
Sumwhyle wyth wodwos þat woned in þe knarreȝ,
Boþe wyth bulleȝ and bereȝ, and boreȝ oþerquyle,
And etayneȝ þat hym anelede of þe heȝe felle;
Nade he ben duȝty and dryȝe, and Dryȝtyn had serued,

out from the castle that day. He made no delay, but went on his way swiftly; he rode by many a wild and wandering path, as I have heard the story say.

Now the knight goes riding through the realm of Logres, Sir Gawain rides in God's name, though no mere game it seemed to him. Often, companionless, he spent the night alone where he found no fitting hospitality awaiting him. He had no company save his horse among the woods and hills, and no one but God to speak with by the way, till he drew very close to north Wales. Keeping all the islands of Anglesey on his left hand, and passing over the fords at the coastal promontories, he crossed over at the Holy Head, till he gained the shore once more in the wilderness of Wirral; few lived there who loved either God or man whole-heartedly. And ever as he rode, he inquired of the people whom he met whether they had heard any talk of a Green Knight of the Green Chapel in any region thereabouts; and they all denied it, saying no, that never in their lives had they seen any man who was of such a colour as green. The knight took unfamiliar paths among many dreary hills; his mood changed many times before he came to see that chapel.

He clambered up many a cliff in strange regions; having wandered far from his friends, he rode as a stranger. At every ford or stream where the knight crossed over, it was a wonder if he did not find a foe facing him, and one so evil and so fierce that he was compelled to fight. The man encountered so many strange things there among the hills, that it would be too difficult to recount the tenth part of them. Sometimes he fought with dragons, and with wolves also, sometimes with forest trolls, who lived in the rocks, with bulls and bears too, and at other times with boars, and ogres who pursued him from the fells above; had he not been bold and unflinching and served God, without doubt he

Douteles he hade ben ded and dreped ful ofte.
For werre wrathed hym not so much, þat wynter was wors,
When þe colde cler water fro þe cloudeȝ schadde,
And fres er hit falle myȝt to þe fale erþe.
Ner slayn wyth þe slete he sleped in his yrnes
Mo nyȝteȝ þen innoghe in naked rokkeȝ,
Þer as claterande fro þe crest þe colde borne renneȝ,
And henged heȝe ouer his hede in hard iisse-ikkles.
Þus in peryl and payne and plytes ful harde
Bi contray caryeȝ þis knyȝt tyl Krystmasse euen,
al one.
Þe knyȝt wel þat tyde
To Mary made his mone,
Þat ho hym red to ryde
And wysse hym to sum wone.

Bi a mounte on þe morne meryly he rydes
Into a forest ful dep, þat ferly watȝ wylde,
Hiȝe hilleȝ on vche a halue, and holtwodeȝ vnder
Of hore okeȝ ful hoge a hundreth togeder;
Þe hasel and þe haȝþorne were harled al samen,
With roȝe raged mosse rayled aywhere,
With mony bryddeȝ vnblyþe vpon bare twyges,
Þat pitosly þer piped for pyne of þe colde.
Þe gome vpon Gryngolet glydeȝ hem vnder,
Þurȝ mony misy and myre, mon al hym one,
Carande for his costes, lest he ne keuer schulde
To se þe seruyse of þat syre, þat on þat self nyȝt
Of a burde watȝ borne oure baret to quelle.
And þerfore sykyng he sayde, 'I beseche þe, lorde,
And Mary, þat is myldest moder so dere,
Of sum herber þer heȝly I myȝt here masse
Ande þy matyneȝ to-morne, mekely I ask,
And þerto prestly I pray my pater and aue
and crede.'
He rode in his prayere
And cryed for his mysdede;
He sayned hym in syþes sere
And sayde, 'Cros Kryst me spede!'

would have been struck down and killed many a time. Yet fighting did not so greatly trouble him, the winter weather was worse, when the cold, clear rain was shed from the clouds, and froze before it could fall on the faded earth. Almost slain by the sleet, he slept in his armour night after night amongst the naked rocks, where the cold burn came crashing down from the cliff-top, and hung high above his head in hard icicles. So through pain and peril and the greatest hardships this knight went riding across the country until Christmas Eve, all alone. Then the knight duly made his prayer to Mary, that she would direct his course and guide him to some dwelling.

On the morning of that day he rode in good heart over a mountain and deep into a forest that was wonderfully wild, with high hills on every side, and woods at their feet of hundreds of great, grey oaks; the hazel and the hawthorn were all tangled together, hung all over with rough, shaggy moss, with many mournful birds upon their bare branches, piping pathetically there, in pain from the cold. The knight upon Gryngolet passed beneath them, through many a bog and mire, a man all alone, concerned about his religious duties, lest he should not manage to see Mass served for the Lord, who on that very night was born of a virgin to end our troubles. And so, sighing, he said, 'I beseech you, Lord, and Mary, your most dear and gentle mother, for some shelter where I may devoutly hear Mass and the matins of your feast day tomorrow, meekly I ask it, and in preparation I here and now recite my Paternoster and Ave Maria and Creed.' He rode on as he prayed and lamented his sins; he crossed himself repeatedly and said, 'Christ's cross be my aid!'

Nade he sayned hymself, segge, bot þrye,
Er he watȝ war in þe wod of a won in a mote,
Abof a launde, on a lawe, loken vnder boȝeȝ
Of mony borelych bole aboute bi þe diches:
A castel þe comlokest þat euer knyȝt aȝte,
Pyched on a prayere, a park al aboute,
With a pyked palays pyned ful þik,
Þat vmbeteȝe mony tre mo þen two myle.
Þat holde on þat on syde þe haþel auysed,
As hit schemered and schon þurȝ þe schyre okeȝ;
Þenne hatȝ he hendly of his helme, and heȝly he þonkeȝ
Jesus and sayn Gilyan, þat gentyle ar boþe,
Þat cortaysly hade hym kydde and his cry herkened.
'Now bone hostel,' coþe þe burne, 'I beseche yow ȝette!'
Þenne gedereȝ he to Gryngolet with þe gilt heleȝ,
And he ful chauncely hatȝ chosen to þe chef gate,
Þat broȝt bremly þe burne to þe bryge ende
in haste.
Þe bryge watȝ breme vpbrayde,
Þe ȝateȝ wer stoken faste,
Þe walleȝ were wel arayed,
Hit dut no wyndeȝ blaste.

Þe burne bode on blonk, þat on bonk houed
Of þe depe double dich þat drof to þe place;
Þe walle wod in þe water wonderly depe,
Ande eft a ful huge heȝt hit haled vpon lofte,
Of harde hewen ston vp to þe tableȝ,
Enbaned vnder þe abataylment, in þe best lawe;
And syþen garyteȝ ful gaye gered bitwene,
Wyth mony luflych loupe þat louked ful clene:
A better barbican þat burne blusched vpon neuer.
And innermore he behelde þat halle ful hyȝe,
Towres telded bytwene, trochet ful þik,
Fayre fylyoleȝ þat fyȝed, and ferlyly long,
With coruon coprounes craftyly sleȝe.
Chalkwhyt chymnees þer ches he innoȝe
Vpon bastel roueȝ, þat blenked ful quyte;
So mony pynakle payntet watȝ poudred ayquere,

785 blonk … bonk: MS bonk … blonk

Scarcely had the knight crossed himself three times, when he became aware of a dwelling in the wood surrounded by a moat, on a knoll above a glade, shut in under the boughs of many massive trees round about the defensive ditches: the fairest castle that ever a knight owned, erected in a meadow, surrounded by a park, set about by a palisade of close-set spikes, which enclosed many trees in its circuit of more than two miles. The knight gazed at the castle from his side of the moat, as it shimmered and shone through the lovely oaks; then he reverently removed his helmet, and devoutly thanked Jesus and St Julian, who are both gracious, for having shown him courtesy and listened to his cry for help. 'Now I beseech you,' said the knight, 'grant me good lodging.' Then he urged on Gryngolet with his gilded spurs, and as he had most fortunately taken the main path, it directly and speedily brought the knight to the end of the drawbridge. The bridge was firmly drawn up, the gates were securely shut, the walls were well constructed and feared no tempest blast.

The knight remained on his horse, which came to a halt on the bank of the deep double ditch which surrounded the building; the wall went down into the water extremely deep, and it also rose up above to a very great height, built of hard cut stone up to the cornices, with courses of masonry projecting under the battlements in the best style; and then elegant turrets constructed at intervals along the wall, with many fine loopholes that were neatly shuttered: a better barbican the knight had never seen. And further in he saw the lofty hall, towers set up here and there, thickly tined, handsome turrets in matching style, and wonderfully tall, with carved tops ingeniously and skilfully made. He perceived there many chimneys pale as chalk gleaming whitely upon the tower roofs; so many painted pinnacles were scattered everywhere,

Among þe castel carnelez clambred so þik,
Þat pared out of papure purely hit semed.
Þe fre freke on þe fole hit fayr innoghe þoȝt,
If he myȝt keuer to com þe cloyster wythinne,
To herber in þat hostel whyl halyday lested,
auinant.
He calde, and sone þer com
A porter pure plesaunt,
On þe wal his ernd he nome,
And haylsed þe knyȝt erraunt.

'Gode sir,' quoþ Gawan, 'woldeȝ þou go myn ernde
To þe heȝ lorde of þis hous, herber to craue?'
'Ȝe, Peter,' quoþ þe porter, 'and purely I trowee
Þat ȝe be, wyȝe, welcum to won quyle yow lykeȝ.'
Þen ȝede þe wyȝe ȝerne and com aȝayn swyþe,
And folke frely hym wyth, to fonge þe knyȝt.
Þay let doun þe grete draȝt and derely out ȝeden,
And kneled doun on her knes vpon þe colde erþe
To welcum þis ilk wyȝ, as worþy hom þoȝt;
Þay ȝolden hym þe brode ȝate, ȝarked vp wyde,
And he hem raysed rekenly and rod ouer þe brygge.
Sere seggeȝ hym sesed by sadel, quel he lyȝt,
And syþen stabeled his stede stif men innoȝe.
Knyȝteȝ and swyereȝ comen doun þenne
For to bryng þis buurne wyth blys into halle;
Quen he hef vp his helme, þer hiȝed innoghe
For to hent hit at his honde, þe hende to seruen;
His bronde and his blasoun boþe þay token.
Þen haylsed he ful hendly þo haþeleȝ vchone,
And mony proud mon þer presed, þat prynce to honour.
Alle hasped in his heȝ wede to halle þay hym wonnen,
Þer fayre fyre vpon flet fersly brenned.
Þenne þe lorde of þe lede louteȝ fro his chambre
For to mete wyth menske þe mon on þe flor.
He sayde, 'Ȝe are welcum to welde as yow lykeȝ
Þat here is; al is yowre awen, to haue at yowre wylle
and welde.'
'Graunt mercy,' quoþ Gawayn,
'Þer Kryst hit yow forȝelde.'

815 ȝerne and com *supplied*

clustering so thickly amongst the embrasures of the castle, that it looked just as if cut out of paper. The noble knight on his horse thought it handsome enough, if only he could manage to get inside the bailey, to lodge in that pleasant dwelling while the holy season lasted. He called aloud, and at once there came a very civil porter, who from the wall inquired his business, and greeted the knight errant.

'Good sir,' said Gawain, 'would you go as my messenger to the noble master of this house to ask for shelter?' 'Yes, by St Peter,' said the porter, 'and I am quite sure that you, sir, will be welcome to remain as long as you please.' Then the man quickly went away and returned at once, and others readily came with him to receive the knight. They let down the great drawbridge and courteously went out and knelt down on their knees on the cold ground to welcome this particular knight in the way which seemed to them fitting; they allowed him to pass through the broad gateway, thrown wide open, and he graciously bid them rise and rode over the drawbridge. Several attendants held his saddle while he dismounted, and then many stalwart grooms led his horse to stable. Knights and squires then came down to bring the knight with rejoicing into the hall; when he lifted off his helmet, many there hastened to take it from his hands, to be of service to the nobleman; they took his sword and his shield also. Then he most courteously greeted each of the knights, and many proud men pressed forward to honour that prince. They brought him, all buckled in his splendid armour, into the hall, where a fine fire burned fiercely upon the hearth. Then the lord of the household came down from his own room to greet the knight graciously in the hall. He said, 'You are welcome to treat everything here as you please; it is all your own, to have and use as you wish.' 'Many thanks,' said Gawain, 'may Christ

As frekeȝ þat semed fayn
Ayþer oþer in armeȝ con felde.

Gawayn glyȝt on þe gome þat godly hym gret,
And þuȝt hit a bolde burne þat þe burȝ aȝte,
A hoge haþel for þe noneȝ, and of hyghe eldee;
Brode, bryȝt watȝ his berde, and al beuer-hwed,
Sturne, stif on þe stryþþe on stalworth schonkeȝ,
Felle face as þe fyre, and fre of hys speche;
And wel hym semed, for soþe, as þe segge þuȝt,
To lede a lortschyp in lee of leudeȝ ful gode.
Þe lorde hym charred to a chambre, and chefly cumaundeȝ
To delyuer hym a leude, hym loȝly to serue;
And þere were boun at his bode burneȝ innoȝe
Þat broȝt hym to a bryȝt boure, þer beddyng watȝ noble,
Of cortynes of clene sylk wyth cler golde hemmeȝ,
And couertoreȝ ful curious with comlych paneȝ
Of bryȝt blaunner aboue, enbrawded bisydeȝ,
Rudeleȝ rennande on ropeȝ, red golde ryngeȝ,
Tapiteȝ tyȝt to þe woȝe, of tuly and tars,
And vnder fete, on þe flet, of folȝande sute.
Þer he watȝ dispoyled, wyth specheȝ of myerþe,
Þe burn of his bruny and of his bryȝt wedeȝ.
Ryche robes ful rad renkkeȝ hym broȝten,
For to charge and to chaunge and chose of þe best.
Sone as he on hent, and happed þerinne,
Þat sete on hym semly, wyth saylande skyrteȝ,
Þe ver by his uisage verayly hit semed
Welneȝ to vche haþel, alle on hwes,
Lowande and lufly, alle his lymmeȝ vnder,
Þat a comloker knyȝt neuer Kryst made,
hem þoȝt.
Wheþen in worlde he were,
Hit semed as he moȝt
Be prynce withouten pere
In felde þer felle men foȝt.

A cheyer byfore þe chemné, þer charcole brenned,
Watȝ grayþed for Sir Gawan grayþely with cloþeȝ,

850 chefly: MS clesly

reward you for this.' Like men of goodwill, they clasped each other in their arms.

Gawain looked at the man who had greeted him courteously, and thought that he who owned the castle was a valiant knight, a huge man, indeed, and of mature age; broad and bright was his beard, and all of a beaver-hue, stern-looking, standing firm on stalwart legs, his face bold as the fire, and frank in his speech; and certainly, so the knight thought, it well befitted him to hold a command over good knights in a castle. The lord conducted him to a private room, and gave particular instructions that a man be assigned to him to serve him humbly; and there were many servants ready at his bidding, who led him into a fair chamber where the trappings of the bed were splendid, hangings of fine silk with bright golden hems, and coverlets of elaborate design with beautiful panels of pure white ermine on them, embroidered at the sides, curtains running on cords through red gold rings, tapestries of Toulouse and Tharsian silk hung on the walls, and others of similar sort on the floor underfoot. There he was disarmed with pleasant talk; the knight was stripped of his coat of mail and his bright raiment. Men promptly brought him splendid robes to select the best for his wearing and change into them. When he had chosen one, and was dressed in it, one that sat on him handsomely with flowing skirts, from his appearance it seemed to everyone really almost like the spring, all his limbs under it all in glowing and delightful colours, so that it seemed to them God had never made a more handsome knight. Whatever part of the world he might be from, it seemed as if he must be a prince without peer on any field where fierce men fought.

Before the fireplace, where charcoal burnt, a chair was promptly prepared for Sir Gawain with coverings, cushions laid upon quilted

Whyssynes vpon queldepoyntes þat koynt wer boþe.
And þenne a meré mantyle watȝ on þat mon cast,
Of a broun bleeaunt, enbrauded ful ryche,
And fayre furred wythinne with felleȝ of þe best,
Alle of ermyn in erde, his hode of þe same.
And he sete in þat settel semlych ryche,
And achaufed hym chefly, and þenne his cher mended.
Sone watȝ telded vp a tabil on tresteȝ ful fayre,
Clad wyth a clene cloþe þat cler quyt schewed,
Sanap and salure and syluerin sponeȝ.
Þe wyȝe wesche at his wylle, and went to his mete.
Seggeȝ hym serued semly innoȝe
Wyth sere sewes and sete, sesounde of þe best,
Double-felde, as hit falleȝ, and fele kyn fischeȝ,
Summe baken in bred, summe brad on þe gledeȝ,
Summe soþen, summe in sewe sauered with spyces,
And ay sawses so sleȝe þat þe segge lyked.
Þe freke calde hit a fest ful frely and ofte
Ful hendely, quen alle þe haþeles rehayted hym at oneȝ
as hende:
'Þis penaunce now ȝe take,
And eft hit schal amende.'
Þat mon much merþe con make,
For wyn in his hed þat wende.

Þenne watȝ spyed and spured vpon spare wyse
Bi preué poynteȝ of þat prynce, put to hymseluen,
Þat he beknew cortaysly of þe court þat he were
Þat aþel Arthure þe hende haldeȝ hym one,
Þat is þe ryche ryal kyng of þe Rounde Table,
And hit watȝ Wawen hymself þat in þat won sytteȝ,
Comen to þat Krystmasse, as case hym þen lymped.
When þe lorde hade lerned þat he þe leude hade,
Loude laȝed he þerat, so lef hit hym þoȝt,
And alle þe men in þat mote maden much joye
To apere in his presence prestly þat tyme
Þat alle prys and prowes and pured þewes
Apendes to hys persoun, and praysed is euer;

884 tabil: MS tapit
893 sawses so sleȝe: MS sawes so sleȝeȝ

cloths, both skilfully made. And then a gay mantle was put upon the knight, of a brown silk, richly embroidered and beautifully furred inside with the best skins, all of real ermine, its hood of the same materials. And he sat down in that rich and handsome seat, and warmed himself quickly, and then his spirits rose. Straightway a table was set up on trestles very neatly, covered with a clean cloth, pure white in colour, and an overcloth, with a salt-cellar, and silver spoons. At his good pleasure the knight washed his hands and sat down to his meal. He was most handsomely served with various excellent broths, seasoned in the best way, in double portions, as was fitting, and many kinds of fish, some baked in pie-crust, some grilled on the embers, some poached, some in stew flavoured with spices, and all with sauces so skilfully made as to please the knight. The knight very readily and repeatedly called it a feast, most politely, whereupon, with equal courtesy, all the company as one man pressed him: 'Accept this penitential fare now, and later it will improve.' The knight was very merry because of the wine which went to his head.

Then questions were asked and inquiries tactfully made of the prince, by discreet queries put to him, until he courteously acknowledged that he was a member of the court ruled in sovereignty by the noble and gracious Arthur, the right royal king of the Round Table, and that it was Gawain himself who was sitting in that hall, having come, as chance would have it, to the Christmas festivities there. When the master of the house had learnt what man he had there, he laughed aloud at the news, so pleasant did it seem to him, and all the people in the castle took great delight in appearing as quickly as possible in his presence to whose person belong all excellence and prowess and refined conduct, and who is praised perpetually, above all mortal men

Byfore alle men vpon molde his mensk is þe most.
Vch segge ful softly sayde to his fere:
'Now schal we semlych se sleȝteȝ of þeweȝ
And þe teccheles termes of talkyng noble;
Wich spede is in speche, vnspurd may we lerne,
Syn we haf fonged þat fyne fader of nurture.
God hatȝ geuen vus his grace godly for soþe,
Þat such a gest as Gawan grаunteȝ vus to haue,
When burneȝ blyþe of his burþe schal sitte
          and synge.
     In menyng of manereȝ mere
     Þis burne now schal vus bryng;
     I hoþe þat may hym here
     Schal lerne of luf-talkyng.'

Bi þat þe diner watȝ done and þe dere vp,
Hit watȝ neȝ at þe niyȝt neȝed þe tyme.
Chaplayneȝ to þe chapeles chosen þe gate,
Rungen ful rychely, ryȝt as þay schulden,
To þe hersum euensong of þe hyȝe tyde.
Þe lorde loutes þerto, and þe lady als;
Into a cumly closet coyntly ho entreȝ.
Gawan glydeȝ ful gay and gos þeder sone;
Þe lorde laches hym by þe lappe and ledeȝ hym to sytte,
And couþly hym knoweȝ and calleȝ hym his nome,
And sayde he watȝ þe welcomest wyȝe of þe worlde;
And he hym þonkked þroly, and ayþer halched oþer,
And seten soberly samen þe seruise quyle.
Þenne lyst þe lady to loke on þe knyȝt,
Þenne com ho of hir closet with mony cler burdeȝ.
Ho watȝ þe fayrest in felle, of flesche and of lyre,
And of compas and colour and costes, of alle oþer,
And wener þen Wenore, as þe wyȝe þoȝt.
Ho ches þurȝ þe chaunsel to cheryche þat hende;
Anoþer lady hir lad bi þe lyft honde,
Þat watȝ alder þen ho, an auncian hit semed,
And heȝly honowred with haþeleȝ aboute.
Bot vnlyke on to loke þo ladyes were,
For if þe ȝonge watȝ ȝep, ȝolȝe watȝ þat oþer;

946 Ho: MS he

his reputation is pre-eminent. Each one said quietly to his neighbour: 'Now we shall have the pleasure of seeing masterly displays of good manners and hearing the polished phrases of courtly discourse; we can learn without inquiry what profit there is in the art of conversation, since we have welcomed here this perfect master of good breeding. God has indeed graciously favoured us, in permitting us to have such a guest as Gawain, at the season when men are to sit singing with joy at His birth. This man will now instruct us in the appreciation of refined behaviour; I believe that whoever has the opportunity of hearing him will learn something of the language of love.'

By the time the meal was finished and the prince had risen, night-time had drawn near. Clerics made their way to the chapels, rang the bells most magnificently, just as they ought, for the solemn evensong of the festive season. The lord came down for it, and the lady also; she gracefully entered a handsome enclosed pew. Gawain very gladly hastened there immediately; the lord, taking him by a fold of his robe and leading him to a seat, greeted him familiarly and called him by his name, saying he was the most welcome man in the world; and he thanked him heartily, they embraced each other, and sat quietly together during the service. Then the lady wished to see the knight, and so she came from her pew with many fair maidens. She was the fairest of all in her person, in body and face, and in figure, complexion and bearing, and lovelier than Guenevere, so the knight thought. She made her way across the chancel graciously to greet that courteous knight; another lady led her by the left hand, who was older than she—an elderly woman, it appeared, and highly honoured by the people present. But the ladies were very different in appearance, for if the young one was fresh, the other was withered; a fine red colouring

Riche red on þat on rayled ayquere,
Rugh ronkled chekeȝ þat oþer on rolled;
Kerchofes of þat on, wyth mony cler perleȝ,
Hir brest and hir bryȝt þrote bare displayed,
Schon schyrer þen snawe þat schedeȝ on hilleȝ;
Þat oþer wyth a gorger watȝ gered ouer þe swyre,
Chymbled ouer hir blake chyn with chalkquyte vayles,
Hir frount folden in sylk, enfoubled ayquere,
Toreted and treleted with tryfleȝ aboute,
Þat noȝt watȝ bare of þat burde bot þe blake broȝes,
Þe tweyne yȝen and þe nase, þe naked lyppeȝ,
And þose were soure to se and sellyly blered;
A mensk lady on molde mon may hir calle,
for Gode!
Hir body watȝ schort and þik,
Hir buttokeȝ balȝ and brode;
More lykkerwys on to lyk
Watȝ þat scho hade on lode.

When Gawayn glyȝt on þat gay þat graciously loked,
Wyth leue laȝt of þe lorde he lent hem aȝaynes;
Þe alder he haylses, heldande ful lowe,
Þe loueloker he lappeȝ a lyttel in armeȝ,
He kysses hir comlyly, and knyȝtly he meleȝ.
Þay kallen hym of aquoyntaunce, and he hit quyk askeȝ
To be her seruaunt sothly, if hemself lyked.
Þay tan hym bytwene hem, wyth talkyng hym leden
To chambre, to chemné, and chefly þay asken
Spyceȝ, þat vnsparely men speded hom to bryng,
And þe wynnelych wyne þerwith vche tyme.
Þe lorde luflych aloft lepeȝ ful ofte,
Mynned merthe to be made vpon mony syþeȝ,
Hent heȝly of his hode, and on a spere henged,
And wayned hom to wynne þe worchip þerof
Þat most myrþe myȝt meue þat Crystenmas whyle.
'And I schal fonde, bi my fayth, to fylter wyth þe best

958 chalkquyte: MS mylkquyte
960 Toreted: MS toret
967 balȝ: MS bay
971 lent: MS went

everywhere adorned the one, rough, wrinkled cheeks hung sagging on the other; the kerchiefs of the one, with many lustrous pearls, exposed her breast and white throat uncovered, shining more brightly than the snow which falls upon the hillsides; the other was clothed about the neck with a wimple, swathed over her swarthy chin with veils white as chalk, her forehead entirely muffled up, enfolded in silk, edged with embroidery and latticed about with ornaments, so that no part of that lady was uncovered save the black eyebrows, the two eyes and the nose, and the naked lips, and they were unpleasant to look at and the eyes very bleared; a lady much honoured in the world, she may truly be called! Her body was short and stout, her hips bulging and broad; more pleasing to the taste was she whom she was leading.

When Gawain set eyes on that beauty, who looked graciously upon him, with the lord's permission he went to meet the ladies; the elder he greets, bowing very low, the fairer he embraces an instant in his arms, politely kissing her and addressing her courteously. They desire his acquaintance, and he instantly begs to be their faithful servant, if they so please. Placing him between them, they conduct him, conversing together, to their sitting-room, to the hearthside, and at once call for sweetmeats, which servants hasten to bring them without stint, and, with each service, cheering wine as well. The lord, often leaping to his feet in friendly fashion, repeatedly urged others to make merry, gaily snatched off his hood, hung it on a spear, and challenged them to win the honour of possessing it, whichever of them could stir up the greatest mirth at that Christmas season. 'And, by my faith, I shall try, with the help of my friends, to compete with the best of you, rather

Er me wont þe wede, with help of my frendeȝ.'
Þus wyth laȝande loteȝ þe lorde hit tayt makeȝ,
For to glade Sir Gawayn with gomneȝ in halle
þat nyȝt,
Til þat hit watȝ tyme
Þe lord comaundet lyȝt;
Sir Gawen his leue con nyme
And to his bed hym diȝt.

On þe morne, as vch mon myneȝ þat tyme
Þat Dryȝtyn for oure destyné to deȝe watȝ borne,
Wele waxeȝ in vche a won in worlde for his sake.
So did hit þere on þat day þurȝ dayntés mony:
Boþe at mes and at mele messes ful quaynt
Derf men vpon dece drest of þe best.
Þe olde auncian wyf heȝest ho sytteȝ;
Þe lorde lufly her by lent, as I trowe.
Gawan and þe gay burde togeder þay seten,
Euen inmyddeȝ, as þe messe metely come,
And syþen þurȝ al þe sale, as hem best semed,
Bi vche grome at his degré grayþely watȝ serued.
Þer watȝ mete, þer watȝ myrþe, þer watȝ much ioye,
Þat for to telle þerof hit me tene were,
And to poynte hit ȝet I pyned me parauenture.
Bot ȝet I wot þat Wawen and þe wale burde
Such comfort of her compaynye caȝten togeder
Þurȝ her dere dalyaunce of her derne wordeȝ,
Wyth clene cortays carp closed fro fylþe,
Þat hor play watȝ passande vche prynce gomen,
in vayres.
Trumpeȝ and nakerys,
Much pypyng þer repayres;
Vche mon tented hys,
And þay two tented þayres.

Much dut watȝ þer dryuen þat day and þat oþer,
And þe þryd as þro þronge in þerafter;
Þe ioye of sayn Joneȝ day watȝ gentyle to here,

987 wede: MS wedeȝ
992 lord: MS kyng

than lose this garment.' So with laughing words the lord made merry, to cheer Sir Gawain with social pastimes that evening, until the time came when the host called for candles; then Sir Gawain took his leave and went to his bed.

On the morrow, when all men commemorate the time when the Lord God was born to die for our good, joy springs up in every dwelling on earth for His sake. So it did there on that day on account of many delights: both at dinner and at other meals, willing servants set out upon the high table dishes of the best, skilfully prepared. The venerable old lady sat in the place of honour; the lord, as I understand, courteously took his seat beside her. Gawain and the fair lady sat together, right in the centre, where the dishes came first, as was proper, and then were served throughout the hall as seemed most fitting to the company, until every man had been duly served according to his rank. There was feasting, there was merry-making, there was much rejoicing, so that it would be difficult for me to convey it, even if, perhaps, I took pains to detail it further. But, nevertheless, I do know that Gawain and the fair lady found such delight in each other's society, from the agreeable intimacy between them in their private talk, with refined and courteous conversation free from impropriety, that truly their recreation was better than any sport of princes. There was much music there of trumpets, pipes and drums; everyone was intent upon his own pleasure, and those two upon theirs.

There was much merry-making there that day and the next, and the third day following was just as intensely crowded with pleasure; the rejoicing on St John's Day was glorious to hear, and that, those present

And watȝ þe last of þe layk, leudeȝ þer þoȝten.
Þer wer gestes to go vpon þe gray morne,
Forþy wonderly þay woke, and þe wyn dronken,
Daunsed ful dreȝly wyth dere caroleȝ.
At þe last, when hit watȝ late, þay lachen her leue,
Vchon to wende on his way þat watȝ wyȝe stronge.
Gawan gef hym god day, þe godmon hym lachcheȝ,
Ledes hym to his awen chambre, þe chymné bysyde,
And þere he draȝeȝ hym on dryȝe, and derely hym þonkkeȝ
Of þe wynne worschip þat he hym wayued hade,
As to honour his hous on þat hyȝe tyde,
And enbelyse his burȝ with his bele chere:
'Iwysse, sir, quyl I leue, me worþeȝ þe better
Þat Gawayn hatȝ ben my gest at Goddeȝ awen fest.'
'Grant merci, sir,' quoþ Gawayn, 'in god fayth hit is yowreȝ,
Al þe honour is your awen—þe heȝe kyng yow ȝelde!
And I am wyȝe at your wylle to worch youre hest,
As I am halden þerto, in hyȝe and in loȝe,
bi riȝt.'
Þe lorde fast can hym payne
To holde lenger þe knyȝt;
To hym answareȝ Gawayn
Bi non way þat he myȝt.

Then frayned þe freke ful fayre at himseluen
Quat derue dede had hym dryuen at þat dere tyme
So kenly fro þe kyngeȝ kourt to kayre al his one,
Er þe halidayeȝ holly were halet out of toun.
'For soþe, sir,' quoþ þe segge, 'ȝe sayn bot þe trawþe;
A heȝe ernde and a hasty me hade fro þo woneȝ,
For I am sumned myselfe to sech to a place,
I ne wot in worlde whederwarde to wende hit to fynde.
I nolde bot if I hit negh myȝt on Nw Ȝeres morne
For alle þe londe inwyth Logres, so me oure lorde help!
Forþy, sir, þis enquest I require yow here,
Þat ȝe me telle with trawþe if euer ȝe tale herde
Of the grene chapel, quere hit on grounde stondeȝ,
And of þe knyȝt þat hit kepes, of colour of grene.
Þer watȝ stabled bi statut a steuen vus bytwene
To mete þat mon at þat mere, ȝif I myȝt last;

1053 ne *supplied*

realised, was the last day of the holiday. The guests were to depart in the grey dawn, and so they revelled late and splendidly, drinking wine and unceasingly singing and dancing pleasant *caroles*. At last, when it was late, they took their leave, ready to go upon their way, all those who were not of the household. When Gawain said goodbye to him, the master of the house, seizing hold of him, led him to his own private room and there, taking him aside near the fireplace, courteously thanked him for the signal mark of respect he had shown him, in honouring his house at that festive season, and gracing his castle with his gracious company: 'Indeed, sir, all my life I shall be the better for the fact that Gawain has been my guest at God's own festival.' 'Many thanks, sir,' said Gawain, 'for, indeed, it is to you they are due, all the honour is on your part—may the Lord above reward you! And I am your man at your command, to do your bidding, as I am duty-bound to do, in all matters, great and small.' The lord earnestly endeavoured to detain the knight longer; Gawain answered him that he could by no means remain.

Then the lord asked him very frankly what dreadful deed had driven him at that festive season from the royal court, riding out so urgently all on his own, before the holy-days had wholly passed. 'Indeed, sir,' said the knight, 'you are only speaking the truth; an important mission and an urgent one has brought me from my abode, for I am required personally to seek out a certain place, and I have not the least idea where to go to find it. I would not for all the land in Logres fail to reach it on New Year's morning, so help me God! Therefore, sir, I make this request of you now, that you tell me truly if ever you heard tell of the Green Chapel, whereabouts it stands, and of the knight, green in colour, who guards it. A tryst was agreed upon by solemn covenant between us, by which I was to meet that man at that appointed place,

And of þat ilk Nw Ȝere bot neked now wonteȝ,
And I wolde loke on þat lede, if God me let wolde,
Gladloker, bi Goddeȝ sun, þen any god welde!
Forþi, iwysse, bi ȝowre wylle, wende me bihoues;
Naf I now to busy bot bare þre dayeȝ,
And me als fayn to falle feye as fayly of myyn ernde.'
Þenne laȝande quoþ þe lorde, 'Now leng þe byhoues,
For I schal teche yow to þat terme bi þe tymeȝ ende,
Þe grene chapayle vpon grounde greue yow no more;
Bot ȝe schal be in yowre bed, burne, at þyn ese,
Quyle forth dayeȝ, and ferk on þe fyrst of þe ȝere,
And cum to þat merk at mydmorn, to make quat yow likeȝ
    in spenne.
  Dowelleȝ whyle New Ȝeres daye,
  And rys and raykeȝ þenne.
  Mon schal yow sette in waye;
  Hit is not two myle henne.'

Þenne watȝ Gawan ful glad, and gomenly he laȝed:
'Now I þonk yow þryuandely þurȝ alle oþer þynge;
Now acheued is my chaunce, I schal at your wylle
Dowelle, and elleȝ do quat ȝe demen.'
Þenne sesed hym þe syre and set hym bysyde,
Let þe ladieȝ be fette to lyke hem þe better.
Þer watȝ seme solace by hemself stille;
Þe lorde let for luf loteȝ so myry,
As wyȝ þat wolde of his wyte, ne wyst quat he myȝt.
Þenne he carped to þe knyȝt, criande loude,
'Ȝe han demed to do þe dede þat I bidde;
Wyl ȝe halde þis hes here at þys oneȝ?'
'Ȝe, sir, for soþe,' sayd þe segge trwe,
'Whyl I byde in yowre borȝe, be bayn to ȝowre hest.'
'For ȝe haf trauayled,' quoþ þe tulk, 'towen fro ferre,
And syþen waked me wyth, ȝe arn not wel waryst
Nauþer of sostnaunce ne of slepe, soþly I knowe.
Ȝe schal lenge in your lofte and lyȝe in your ese
To-morn quyle þe messequyle, and to mete wende
When ȝe wyl, wyth my wyf, þat wyth yow schal sitte
And comfort yow with companyny, til I to cort torne.
    Ȝe lende,

if I should live till then; and it now wants only a little time to New Year itself, and, if God should permit me, I would rather, by Christ, set eyes on that man than possess any treasure, no matter what! And so, indeed, by your leave, I am obliged to go; I have now a mere three days to be about my business, and I would rather be struck down dead than fail in my mission.' Then, laughing, the lord said, 'Now you *must* stay, for I shall direct you to the appointed place by the end of that period, so let the whereabouts of the Green Chapel trouble you no more; but rather you shall lie in your bed, sir, at your ease, until late in the day, and leave on the first day of the year, and reach the appointed place at mid-morning, to do whatever you wish there. Stay here until New Year's Day, and then get up and go. You shall be set upon the road; the place is not two miles from here.'

Then Gawain was very glad and he laughed merrily: 'Now I thank you heartily for this above everything else; since my adventure is almost accomplished I shall stay, as you request, and in other matters do whatever you think fit.' Then the lord took him and seated him at his side, and caused the ladies to be fetched for their greater pleasure. They had excellent enjoyment by themselves in privacy; the lord, in his delight, made such merry speeches, like a man who was about to take leave of his senses and knew not what he was doing. Then he said to the knight, speaking aloud, 'You have agreed to do whatever I ask; will you keep that promise here and now?' 'Yes, sir, certainly,' said the knight, true to his word, 'while I remain in your castle, I shall be obedient to your command.' 'As you have had a hard journey coming from afar,' said the lord, 'and then stayed awake all night with me, you are not yet fully refreshed either by food or sleep, I know quite well. You shall stay in your room, and lie at your ease tomorrow morning until time for Mass, and come to table whenever you like, with my wife, who shall sit with you and amuse you with her company, till I

And I schal erly ryse,
On huntyng wyl I wende.'
Gauayn grantez alle þyse,
Hym heldande, as þe hende.

'Ȝet firre,' quoþ þe freke, 'a forwarde we make:
Quat-so-euer I wynne in þe wod hit worþez to yourez,
And quat chek so ȝe acheue chaunge me þerforne.
Swete, swaþ we so—sware with trawþe—
Queþer, leude, so lymp, lere oþer better.'
'Bi God,' quoþ Gawayn þe gode, 'I grant þertylle;
And þat yow lyst for to layke, lef hit me þynkes.'
'Who bryngez vus þis beuerage, þis bargayn is maked,'
So sayde þe lorde of þat lede; þay laȝed vchone,
Þay dronken and daylyeden and dalten vntyȝtel,
Þise lordez and ladyez, quyle þat hem lyked.
And syþen with frenkysch fare and fele fayre lotez
Þay stoden and stemed and stylly speken,
Kysten ful comlyly and kaȝten her leue.
With mony leude ful lyȝt and lemande torches
Vche burne to his bed watz broȝt at þe laste,
ful softe.
To bed ȝet er þay ȝede,
Recorded couenauntez ofte;
Þe olde lorde of þat leude
Cowþe wel halde layk alofte.

III

Ful erly bifore þe day þe folk vprysen,
Gestes þat go wolde hor gromez þay calden,
And þay busken vp bilyue blonkkez to sadel,
Tyffen her takles, trussen her males;
Richen hem þe rychest, to ryde alle arayde,
Lepen vp lyȝtly, lachen her brydeles,
Vche wyȝe on his way þer hym wel lyked.
Þe leue lorde of þe londe watz not þe last
Arayed for þe rydyng, with renkkez ful mony;
Ete a sop hastyly, when he hade herde masse,

return home. You stay here, and I will rise early; I mean to go hunting.' Gawain agreed to all this, bowing, like the courteous man he was.

'Moreover,' said the lord, 'let us make an agreement: whatever I take in the woods shall become yours, and whatever good or ill you gain here, give it to me in exchange for that. Good sir, let us exchange in this way—swear it honestly—whether, sir, we gain or lose by it.' 'Before God,' said the good Sir Gawain, 'I agree to that; if you are pleased to sport so, I am perfectly content.' 'If someone will bring us the drink to seal it, the bargain is made,' so said the lord of the household; they all laughed, they drank and chatted and behaved without constraint, these lords and ladies, for as long as they pleased. And then with elaborate courtesy and many polite speeches they stood up and lingered still, talking quietly, kissed ceremoniously and took their leave. With many a brisk serving-man and with gleaming torches everyone was finally conducted quietly to his bed. But before they went to bed, they frequently repeated the terms of the agreement; he who had long been lord of that company well knew how to keep up the sport.

III

Very early, before the dawn, the company get up, guests who wish to leave call their servants, and they quickly hasten to saddle the horses, prepare their gear, pack their bags; the nobles dress themselves, in readiness to ride, mount swiftly, seize their bridles, each one going on his way where he best pleased. The good lord of that land was not the last to be ready for riding, with many followers; when he had heard Mass, he ate a morsel hurriedly, and to the sound of a horn sped in

With bugle to bent-felde he buskeȝ bylyue.
By þat any daylyȝt lemed vpon erþe,
He with his haþeles on hyȝe horsses weren.
Þenne þise cacheres þat couþe cowpled hor houndeȝ,
Vnclosed þe kenel dore and calde hem þeroute,
Blwe bygly in bugleȝ þre bare mote.
Braches bayed þerfore and breme noyse maked,
And þay chastysed and charred on chasyng þat went,
A hundreth of hunteres, as I haf herde telle,
of þe best.
To trystors vewters ȝod,
Couples huntes of kest;
Þer ros for blasteȝ gode
Gret rurd in þat forest.

At þe fyrst quethe of þe quest quaked þe wylde;
Der drof in þe dale, doted for drede,
Hiȝed to þe hyȝe, bot heterly þay were
Restayed with þe stablye, þat stoutly ascryed.
Þay let þe hertteȝ haf þe gate, with þe hyȝe hedes,
Þe breme bukkeȝ also with hor brode paumeȝ;
For þe fre lorde hade defende in fermysoun tyme
Þat þer schulde no mon meue to þe male dere.
Þe hindeȝ were halden in, with 'hay!' and 'war!',
Þe does dryuen with gret dyn to þe depe sladeȝ.
Þer myȝt mon se, as þay slypte, slentyng of arwes;
At vche wende vnder wande wapped a flone,
Þat bigly bote on þe broun, with ful brode hedeȝ.
What! þay brayen and bleden, bi bonkkeȝ þay deȝen,
And ay rachches in a res radly hem folȝes,
Huntereȝ wyth hyȝe horne hasted hem after
Wyth such a crakkande kry as klyffes haden brusten.
What wylde so atwaped wyȝes þat schotten
Watȝ al toraced and rent at þe resayt,
Bi þay were tened at þe hyȝe, and taysed to þe wattreȝ;
Þe ledeȝ were so lerned at þe loȝe trysteres,
And þe grehoundeȝ so grete, þat geten hem bylyue
And hem tofylched, as fast as frekeȝ myȝt loke,
þer-ryȝt.
Þe lorde for blys abloy

haste to the hunting-field. By the time some daylight shone upon the earth, he and his men were on their tall steeds. Then the huntsmen, who knew their duty, leashed their hounds in pairs, opened the kennel door and called them out, loudly sounding on their horns three single notes. At that the hounds bayed, and made a fierce din, and those that went chasing off were whipped in and turned back by a host of huntsmen, most highly skilled, so I have heard tell. Keepers of hounds went to their hunting stations, huntsmen cast off the leashes; at their splendid sounding there arose a great commotion in the forest.

At the first utterance of the baying hounds all wild creatures trembled; deer rushed along the valley, crazed with fear, quickly making for the higher ground, but suddenly they were checked by the ring of beaters, who shouted vigorously. They let the stags, with their splendid heads, pass by, the stout bucks also with their broad antlers; for the noble lord had forbidden that anyone should start or rouse the male deer in the close season. The hinds were held back, with shouts of 'hey!' and 'ware!', the does were driven down with great clamour to the deep dales. There might one see, as they glanced past, the slanting flight of arrows; at each turning in the wood a shaft shot out, their broad heads biting deeply into the brown hides. Ah! they roar and bleed, dying on the hillsides, hounds forever following them in a headlong rush, huntsmen with loud horns hastening after them with a resounding cry as if the rocks were splitting. Any beasts that escaped the bowmen were all pulled down and slaughtered at the receiving stations, having been hounded from the high ground and driven down to the streams; the men at the lower stations were so skilled, and the greyhounds so large, that they seized them instantly and pulled them down on the spot, in the twinkling of an eye. The lord, beside himself with delight, galloped

Ful oft con launce and lyȝt,
And drof þat day wyth joy
Thus to þe derk nyȝt.

Þus laykeȝ þis lorde by lynde-wodeȝ eueȝ,
And Gawayn þe god mon in gay bed lygeȝ,
Lurkkeȝ quyl þe daylyȝt lemed on þe wowes,
Vnder couertour ful clere, cortyned aboute.
And as in slomeryng he slode, sleȝly he herde
A littel dyn at his dor, and dernly vpon;
And he heueȝ vp his hed out of þe cloþes,
A corner of þe cortyn he caȝt vp a lyttel,
And wayteȝ warly þiderwarde quat hit be myȝt.
Hit watȝ þe ladi, loflyest to beholde,
Þat droȝ þe dor after hir ful dernly and stylle,
And boȝed towarde þe bed; and þe burne schamed,
And layde hym doun lystyly and let as he slepte.
And ho stepped stilly and stel to his bedde,
Kest vp þe cortyn and creped withinne,
And set hir ful softly on þe bed-syde,
And lenged þere selly longe to loke quen he wakened.
Þe lede lay lurked a ful longe quyle,
Compast in his concience to quat þat cace myȝt
Meue oþer amount—to meruayle hym þoȝt;
Bot ȝet he sayde in hymself, 'More semly hit were
To aspye wyth my spelle in space quat ho wolde.'
Þen he wakenede, and wroth, and to hir warde torned,
And vnlouked his yȝe-lyddeȝ, and let as hym wondered,
And sayned hym, as bi his saȝe þe sauer to worthe,
with hande.
Wyth chynne and cheke ful swete,
Boþe quit and red in blande,
Ful lufly con ho lete
Wyth lyppeȝ smal laȝande.

'God moroun, Sir Gawayn,' sayde þat gay lady,
'Ȝe ar a sleper vnslyȝe, þat mon may slyde hider.
Now ar ȝe tan as-tyt! Bot true vus may schape,

1183 dernly: MS derfly
1208 gay: MS fayr

ahead and dismounted again and again, and so passed the day in pleasure till the dark of night.

So the lord went sporting along the borders of the wood, and the good knight Gawain lay in a fair bed, dozing until the light of day gleamed on the walls, under a bright coverlet, curtained round about. And as he drifted in and out of sleep, he half heard a little noise at his door, and heard it stealthily open; and raising his head up out of the bedclothes, he lifted up a corner of the curtain slightly, and glanced cautiously in that direction to see what it could be. It was the lady, most beautiful to behold, who shut the door behind her very stealthily and quietly, and turned towards the bed; and the knight was embarrassed, and lay down artfully and pretended to be asleep. And she, stepping softly, stole up to his bed, lifted up the curtain and crept inside, and seated herself very gently on the bedside, and remained there a long while to see when he would waken. The knight lay lurking a very long time, turning over in his mind what this state of affairs might portend or signify—it seemed to him very strange; but yet he said to himself, 'It would be more fitting to find out by asking immediately what she wants.' Then he awakened, and stretched himself, and turned towards her, and opened his eyelids, and, feigning to be surprised, crossed himself with his hand, as if by his prayer to protect himself. With white and red mingling in her lovely face, she spoke most amiably with slender laughing lips.

'Good morning, Sir Gawain,' said that fair lady, 'you are a careless sleeper, that one can steal in here. Now, in a trice, you are captured!

I schal bynde yow in your bedde, þat be ȝe trayst':
Al laȝande þe lady lanced þo bourdeȝ.
'Goud moroun, gay,' quoþ Gawayn þe blyþe,
'Me schal worþe at your wille, and þat me wel lykeȝ,
For I ȝelde me ȝederly and ȝeȝe after grace;
And þat is þe best, be my dome, for me byhoueȝ nede':
And þus he bourded aȝayn with mony a blyþe laȝter.
'Bot wolde ȝe, lady louely, þen leue me grante,
And deprece your prysoun, and pray hym to ryse,
I wolde boȝe of þis bed and busk me better;
I schulde keuer þe more comfort to karp yow wyth.'
'Nay, for soþe, beau sir,' sayd þat swete,
'Ȝe schal not rise of your bedde, I rych yow better:
I schal happe yow here þat oþer half als,
And syþen karp wyth my knyȝt þat I kaȝt haue.
For I wene wel, iwysse, Sir Wowen ȝe are,
Þat alle þe worlde worchipeȝ quere-so ȝe ride;
Your honour, your hendelayk is hendely praysed
With lordeȝ, wyth ladyes, with alle þat lyf bere.
And now ȝe ar here, iwysse, and we bot oure one;
My lorde and his ledeȝ ar on lenþe faren,
Oþer burneȝ in her bedde, and my burdeȝ als,
Þe dor drawen and dit with a derf haspe.
And syþen I haue in þis hous hym þat al lykeȝ,
I schal ware my whyle wel, quyl hit lasteȝ,
with tale.
Ȝe ar welcum to my cors,
Yowre awen won to wale;
Me behoueȝ of fyne force
Your seruaunt be, and schale.'

'In god fayth,' quoþ Gawayn, 'gayn hit me þynkkeȝ,
Þaȝ I be not now he þat ȝe of speken;
To reche to such reuerence as ȝe reherce here
I am wyȝe vnworþy, I wot wel myseluen.
Bi God, I were glad and yow god þoȝt
At saȝe oþer at seruyce þat I sette myȝt
To þe plesaunce of your prys—hit were a pure ioye.'
'In god fayth, Sir Gawayn,' quoþ þe gay lady,
'Þe prys and þe prowes þat pleseȝ al oþer,

Unless we can arrange a truce between us, I shall confine you in your bed, be sure of that': laughingly the lady threw out these jests. 'Good morning, fair lady,' said Gawain brightly, 'you shall do with me as you please, and I am quite content, for I yield myself at once and appeal for mercy; and that is the best thing to do, in my opinion, since I must of necessity': and so he jested in reply with many a merry laugh. 'But if you, lovely lady, would now grant me leave, and release your prisoner, and ask him to rise, I would like to leave this bed and dress myself more suitably; I should have all the more pleasure in talking with you.' No, indeed, fair sir,' said the lovely lady, 'you shall not rise from your bed, I have a better plan for you: I shall tuck you in here on the other side as well, and then converse with my knight whom I have caught. For, indeed, I know very well you are Sir Gawain, whom all the world reveres wherever you ride; your honour, your courtly reputation are handsomely praised by lords and ladies, by all men whatsoever. And now you are actually here, and we are quite by ourselves; my husband and his men have gone far away, other folk are in their beds, and my ladies as well, the door is closed and fastened with a stout bar. And since I have in this house the man who pleases everyone, I shall spend my time well, while it lasts, in conversation. To me you are very welcome, and may do just as you wish; I am perforce in duty bound to be your servant, and I shall be so.'

'Really and truly,' said Gawain, 'this seems to me very agreeable, even though I may not be now the man you speak of; I am unworthy to attain to such an honour as you have just mentioned, I myself know very well. Truly, I should be glad if you thought fit that I should devote myself by word or deed to doing your ladyship's pleasure—it would be a sheer joy.' 'Really and truly, Sir Gawain,' said the fair lady, 'if I disparaged or valued lightly the excellence and the prowess that

If I hit lakked oþer set at lyȝt, hit were littel daynté.
Bot hit ar ladyes innoȝe þat leuer wer nowþe
Haf þe, hende, in hor holde, as I þe habbe here,
To daly with derely your daynté wordeȝ,
Keuer hem comfort and colen her care3,
Þen much of þe garysoun oþer golde þat þay hauen.
Bot I louue þat ilk lorde þat þe lyfte haldeȝ,
I haf hit holly in my honde þat al desyres,
            þurȝe grace.'
      Scho made hym so gret chere,
      Þat watȝ so fayr of face;
      Þe knyȝt with speches skere
      Answared to vche a cace.

'Madame,' quoþ þe myry mon, 'Mary yow ȝelde,
For I haf founden, in god fayth, yowre fraunchis nobele;
And oþer ful much of oþer folk fongen hor dedeȝ,
Bot þe daynté þat þay delen for my disert nys euer—
Hit is þe worchyp of yourself þat noȝt bot wel conneȝ.'
'Bi Mary,' quoþ þe menskful, 'me þynk hit an oþer;
For were I worth al þe wone of wymmen alyue,
And al þe wele of þe worlde were in my honde,
And I schulde chepen and chose to cheue me a lorde,
For þe costes þat I haf knowen vpon þe, knyȝt, here,
Of bewté and debonerté and blyþe semblaunt,
And þat I haf er herkkened and halde hit here trwee,
Þer schulde no freke vpon folde bifore yow be chosen.'
'Iwysse, worþy,' quoþ þe wyȝe, 'ȝe haf waled wel better;
Bot I am proude of þe prys þat ȝe put on me,
And, soberly your seruaunt, my souerayn I holde yow,
And yowre knyȝt I becom, and Kryst yow forȝelde.'
Þus þay meled of muchquat til mydmorn paste,
And ay þe lady let lyk as hym loued mych;
Þe freke ferde with defence, and feted ful fayre.
Þaȝ ho were burde bryȝtest þe burne in mynde hade,
Þe lasse luf in his lode for lur þat he soȝt
            boute hone,
      Þe dunte þat schulde hym deue,

1266 nys euer: MS nyseu
1281 as hym: MS ahȳ   1283 ho … burne: MS I … burde

please everyone else, that would be scant courtesy. For there are many ladies who would rather have you, dear sir, in their power now, as I have you here, to exchange agreeable pleasantries in delightful conversation with you, find solace for themselves and assuage their longings, than much of the treasure or gold that they possess. But I thank the Lord who rules the heavens, I have what all desire utterly in my power, by His grace.' She who was so fair of face behaved most graciously to him; the knight responded to each remark with impeccable replies.

'Madam,' said that happy man, 'may Mary reward you, for, truly, I have found in you a noble generosity; and some people take their line of conduct very much from others, but the honour that such people accord me is by no means due to my merit—it is rather to your own credit that you can only behave generously.' 'By Mary,' said the noble lady, 'it seems quite otherwise to me; for were I the equal of all the multitude of mortal women, and all the wealth of the world were in my hands, and I could bargain and select in finding a husband for myself, because of the qualities which I have recognised in you here, sir knight, handsomeness and courtesy and pleasant demeanour, and which I have heard of before and now find to be true, no man on earth would be chosen in preference to you.' 'Indeed, noble lady,' said the knight, 'you have already chosen much better; but I am proud of the value which you set on me, and I, your servant in all earnest, consider you my liege lady, and acknowledge myself your knight, and may Christ reward you.' So they talked of many things until mid-morning was past, and all the time the lady behaved as if she loved him greatly; the knight acted with constraint and behaved most politely. Though she was the fairest woman the knight had ever known, the less warmth there was in his manner because of the fate that he was going to without respite, the blow that was to strike him down, and must

And nedeȝ hit most be done.
Þe lady þenn spek of leue;
He granted hir ful sone.

Þenne ho gef hym god day, and wyth a glent laȝed,
And as ho stod, ho stonyed hym wyth ful stor wordeȝ:
'Now he þat spedeȝ vche spech þis disport ȝelde yow!
Bot þat ȝe be Gawan, hit gotȝ not in mynde.'
'Querfore?' quoþ þe freke, and freschly he askeȝ,
Ferde lest he hade fayled in fourme of his castes.
Bot þe burde hym blessed, and 'Bi þis skyl' sayde:
'So god as Gawayn gaynly is halden,
And cortaysye is closed so clene in hymseluen,
Couth not lyȝtly haf lenged so long wyth a lady
Bot he had craued a cosse bi his courtaysye,
Bi sum towch of summe tryfle at sum taleȝ ende.'
Þen quoþ Wowen, 'Iwysse, worþe as yow lykeȝ;
I schal kysse at your comaundement, as a knyȝt falleȝ,
And fire, lest he displese yow, so plede hit no more.'
Ho comes nerre with þat, and cacheȝ hym in armeȝ,
Louteȝ luflych adoun and þe leude kysseȝ.
Þay comly bykennen to Kryst ayþer oþer;
Ho dos hir forth at þe dore withouten dyn more,
And he ryches hym to ryse and rapes hym sone,
Clepes to his chamberlayn, choses his wede,
Boȝeȝ forth, quen he watȝ boun, blyþely to masse.
And þenne he meued to his mete þat menskly hym keped,
And made myry al day til þe mone rysed,
with game.
Watȝ neuer freke fayrer fonge
Bitwene two so dyngne dame,
Þe alder and þe ȝonge;
Much solace set þay same.

And ay þe lorde of þe londe is lent on his gamneȝ,
To hunt in holteȝ and heþe at hyndeȝ barayne.
Such a sowme he þer slowe bi þat þe sunne heldet,
Of dos and of oþer dere, to deme were wonder.
Þenne fersly þay flokked in folk at þe laste,

1293 not *supplied*

inevitably be struck. At last the lady spoke of taking leave; he consented instantly.

Then she bade him good day, glancing at him with a laugh, and as she stood up, she shocked him with very harsh words: 'Now may He who blesses every conversation reward you for this entertainment! But that you are Gawain is hard to believe.' 'Why so?' said the knight, and he asked anxiously, afraid lest he had been at fault in the way he had spoken. But the lady gave him her blessing, and said: 'For this reason: anyone so perfect as Gawain is rightly held to be, and in whom courtliness is so completely embodied, could not have remained so long with a lady without begging a kiss out of his courtesy, by a hint of some trifling kind at the end of a speech.' Then Gawain said, 'Certainly, be it as you please; I shall kiss at your command, and more, as befits a knight to do, lest he displease you, so urge it no further.' At that she comes closer, and takes him in her arms, lovingly bends down and kisses the knight. Graciously they commend each other to Christ; she goes out of the door without another sound, and he prepares at once to rise, hastening himself, calls to his body-servant, selects his clothes, and, when ready, goes out with an easy mind to Mass. And afterwards he went to his meal which, as was proper, awaited him, and made merry all day, diverting himself, till the moon rose. Never was knight better entertained by two such worthy ladies, the older and the younger; they found great pleasure in each other's company.

And all this time the lord of that land was occupied with his sport, hunting the barren hinds in woods and heathland. By the time the sun declined towards the west, he had slain there such a number of does and other deer that it would be marvellous to relate. Then at the end the hunt eagerly came flocking in, and quickly they made a collection

And quykly of þe quelled dere a querré þay maked.
Þe best boȝed þerto with burneȝ innoghe,
Gedered þe grattest of gres þat þer were,
And didden hem derely vndo as þe dede askeȝ;
Serched hem at þe asay summe þat þer were,
Two fyngeres þay fonde of þe fowlest of alle.
Syþen þay slyt þe slot, sesed þe erber,
Schaued wyth a scharp knyf, and þe schyre knitten.
Syþen rytte þay þe foure lymmes and rent of þe hyde,
Þen brek þay þe balé, þe boweleȝ out token
Lystily for laucyng þe lere of þe knot.
Þay gryped to þe gargulun, and grayþely departed
Þe wesaunt fro þe wynt-hole, and walt out þe gutteȝ.
Þen scher þay out þe schuldereȝ with her scharp knyueȝ,
Haled hem by a lyttel hole to haue hole sydes.
Siþen britned þay þe brest and brayden hit in twynne,
And eft at þe gargulun bigyneȝ on þenne,
Ryueȝ hit vp radly ryȝt to þe byȝt,
Voydeȝ out þe avanters, and verayly þerafter
Alle þe rymeȝ by þe rybbeȝ radly þay lance.
So ryde þay of by resoun bi þe rygge boneȝ,
Euenden to þe haunche, þat henged alle samen,
And heuen hit vp al hole and hwen hit of þere—
And þat þay neme for þe noumbles bi nome, as I trowe,
bi kynde.
Bi þe byȝt al of þe þyȝes
Þe lappeȝ þay lance bihynde;
To hewe hit in two þay hyȝes,
Bi þe bakbon to vnbynde.

Boþe þe hede and þe hals þay hwen of þenne,
And syþen sunder þay þe sydeȝ swyft fro þe chyne,
And þe corbeles fee þay kest in a greue;
Þenn þurled þay ayþer þik side þurȝ bi þe rybbe,
And henged þenne ayþer bi hoȝes of þe fourcheȝ,
Vche freke for his fee, as falleȝ for to haue.
Vpon a felle of þe fayre best fede þay þayr houndes

1333 boweleȝ: MS baleȝ
1334 þe (*1st*): MS &
1357 ayþer: MS aþer

of the slaughtered deer. The nobles with many attendants went up to it, selected the fattest that were there, and had them cut open neatly as the business should be done; some of those present examined them at the 'assay', and found two fingersbreadths of fat on the poorest of the lot. Then they slit the hollow at the base of the throat, took hold of the gullet, scraped it free with a sharp knife, and tied up the gut. Next they cut off the four legs and stripped off the hide, then they opened the belly, took the bowels out deftly so as not to loosen the fastening of the knot. They laid hold of the throat, and swiftly separated the gullet from the windpipe, and tossed out the guts. Then they cut out the shoulder joints with their sharp knives, drawing them through a small hole in order to keep the sides intact. Next they slit open the breast and pulled it apart, and then began upon the throat next, quickly ripping it up right to the fork, clearing out the offal, and immediately afterwards they swiftly severed the membranes on the ribs. In the same way they cleared away neatly along the bones of the back, trimming down to the haunch, so that it all hung together, and lifted it up all in one piece and cut it off there—and that is what they properly call the numbles, I believe; they cut the loose folds of skin at the fork of the thighs; they made haste to hew the carcass in two, dividing it all along the backbone.

They next cut off both the head and the neck, and then they rapidly separated the flanks from the chine, and they tossed the raven's portion into a thicket; next they pierced through both the thick sides at the ribs, and then hung each up by the hocks of the legs, each man receiving as his portion what was due to him. On the hide of the fine

Wyth þe lyuer and þe lyȝteȝ, þe leþer of þe paunche3,
And bred baþed in blod blende þeramongeȝ.
Baldely þay blw prys, bayed þayr rachcheȝ,
Syþen fonge þay her flesche, folden to home,
Strakande ful stoutly mony stif moteȝ.
Bi þat þe daylyȝt watȝ done, þe douthe watȝ al wonen
Into þe comly castel, þer þe knyȝt bideȝ
        ful stille,
    Wyth blys and bryȝt fyr bette.
    Þe lorde is comen þertylle;
    When Gawayn wyth hym mette,
    Þer watȝ bot wele at wylle.

Thenne comaunded þe lorde in þat sale to samen alle þe meny,
Boþe þe ladyes on loghe to lyȝt with her burdes.
Bifore alle þe folk on þe flette, frekeȝ he beddeȝ
Verayly his venysoun to fech hym byforne;
And al godly in gomen Gawayn he called,
Techeȝ hym to þe tayles of ful tayt bestes,
Scheweȝ hym þe schyree grece schorne vpon rybbes.
'How payeȝ yow þis play? Haf I prys wonnen?
Haue I þryuandely þonk þurȝ my craft serued?'
'Ȝe iwysse,' quoþ þat oþer wyȝe, 'here is wayth fayrest
Þat I seȝ þis seuen ȝere in sesoun of wynter.'
'And al I gif yow, Gawayn,' quoþ þe gome þenne,
'For by acorde of couenaunt ȝe craue hit as your awen.'
'Þis is soth,' quoþ þe segge, 'I say yow þat ilke:
Þat I haf worthyly wonnen þis woneȝ wythinne,
Iwysse with as god wylle hit worþeȝ to ȝoureȝ.'
He hasppeȝ his fayre hals his armeȝ wythinne,
And kysses hym as comlyly as he couþe awyse:
'Tas yow þere my cheuicaunce, I cheued no more;
I wowche hit saf fynly, þaȝ feler hit were.'
'Hit is god,' quoþ þe godmon, 'grant mercy þerfore.
Hit may be such hit is þe better, and ȝe me breue wolde
Where ȝe wan þis ilk wele bi wytte of yorseluen.'
'Þat watȝ not forward,' quoþ he, 'frayst me no more;

1386 wonnen *supplied*
1389 he: MS ho
1394 yor-: MS hor-

beast they fed their hounds with the liver and the lights, the lining of the stomachs, and bread soaked in blood mixed with these. Vigorously they blew the kill, and their hounds bayed, then they took their meat, and made for home, proudly sounding many loud calls upon their horns. By the time the daylight had gone, the party had all come home to the fair castle, where the knight has quietly remained, in great contentment and with a bright fire burning. The lord has come to the fireside; when Gawain met him, there was all the happiness that could be desired.

Then the lord commands all the household to gather in the hall, and both the ladies to come down with their maidens. In the presence of the whole company in the hall, he duly orders his men to bring his venison before him; and calling Gawain all in good sport, laughingly directs his attention to the tally of very well grown beasts, pointing out the fine flesh cut from the ribs. 'How like you this sport? Do I deserve praise? Have I thoroughly earned your gratitude by my skill?' 'Yes, indeed,' said the other knight, 'this is the finest kill I have seen these seven years in the winter season.' 'And I give it all to you, Gawain,' said the man then, 'for by the terms of the agreement you may claim it as your own.' 'That is true,' said the knight, 'and I say the same to you: what I have honourably gained in this house shall indeed be yours with as good a will.' Clasping his handsome neck in his arms, and kissing him as gracefully as he could contrive: 'There, take my winnings, I gained nothing else; I give it freely, as I would even were it more.' 'It is excellent,' said the master of the house, 'many thanks for it. It may so be that it is the better prize, if you would only tell me where you gained this treasure by your own skill.' 'That was not in the agreement,' said he, 'so ask me no more; since you have received what is due

For ȝe haf tan þat yow tydeȝ, trawe non oþer
ȝe mowe.'
Þay laȝed and made hem blyþe
Wyth loteȝ þat were to lowe;
To soper þay ȝede as-swyþe,
Wyth dayntés nwe innowe.

And syþen by þe chymné in chamber þay seten,
Wyȝeȝ þe walle wyn weȝed to hem oft,
And efte in her bourdyng þay bayþen in þe morn
To fylle þe same forwardeȝ þat þay byfore maden:
Wat chaunce so bytydeȝ hor cheuysaunce to chaunge,
What nweȝ so þay nome, at naȝt quen þay metten.
Þay acorded of þe couenaunteȝ byfore þe court alle—
Þe beuerage watȝ broȝt forth in bourde at þat tyme—
Þenne þay louelych leȝten leue at þe last,
Vche burne to his bedde busked bylyue.
Bi þat þe coke hade crowen and cakled bot þryse,
Þe lorde watȝ lopen of his bedde, þe leudeȝ vchone,
So þat þe mete and þe masse watȝ metely delyuered,
Þe douthe dressed to þe wod, er any day sprenged,
to chace.
Heȝ with hunte and horneȝ
Þurȝ playneȝ þay passe in space,
Vncoupled among þo þorneȝ
Racheȝ þat ran on race.

Sone þay calle of a quest in a ker syde;
Þe hunt rehayted þe houndeȝ þat hit fyrst mynged,
Wylde wordeȝ hym warp wyth a wrast noyce.
Þe howndeȝ þat hit herde hastid þider swyþe,
And fellen as fast to þe fuyt, fourty at ones.
Þenne such a glauer ande glam of gedered rachcheȝ
Ros þat þe rochereȝ rungen aboute;
Hunterez hem hardened with horne and wyth muthe.
Þen al in a semblé sweyed togeder,
Bitwene a flosche in þat fryth and a foo cragge.
In a knot bi a clyffe, at þe kerre syde,

1396 trawe: MS trawe ȝe
1406 Wat: MS þat

to you, you can expect nothing else.' They laughed and made merry with admirable talk; they went at once to supper, where they had fresh delicacies in plenty.

And then they sat by the fireplace in a private room, servants repeatedly bringing them choice wine, and amid their jesting they again agreed to fulfil next day the same terms they had previously observed: come what may to exchange their winnings, whatever new thing they had gained, when they met at night. They confirmed the terms of the compact before the whole court—at which point the pledging-cup was brought in amid jesting—then at last they took leave of each other courteously, and everyone went quickly to his bed. Before the cock had crowed and cackled more than three times, the lord had leapt from his bed, and all his men, so that the Mass and the meal were duly finished, and the company bound for the forest, to the hunt, before the day dawned. With loud clamour of huntsmen and horns they soon traversed the fields, and among the thorns unleashed the hounds, who rushed away pell-mell.

Soon they gave tongue on finding scent at the edge of a marsh; the huntsmen urged on the hounds who first gave notice of it, shouting excited calls to them with a loud clamour. The hounds who heard it quickly rushed up, and rallied to the trail as fast as they could, forty in a pack. Then such a babble and din rose from the assembled hounds that the rocky hillsides round about echoed; the hunters encouraged them with horn and voice. Then they rushed together all in a pack, between a pool in the wood and a forbidding crag. In a thicket beside a cliff, at the edge of a marsh, where the rugged hillside had tumbled

Þer as þe rogh rocher vnrydely watȝ fallen,
Þay ferden to þe fyndyng, and frekeȝ hem after.
Þay vmbekesten þe knarre and þe knot boþe,
Wyȝeȝ, whyl þay wysten wel wythinne hem hit were,
Þe best þat þer breued watȝ wyth þe blodhoundeȝ.
Þenne þay beten on þe buskeȝ, and bede hym vpryse,
And he vnsoundyly out soȝt seggeȝ ouerþwert;
On þe sellokest swyn swenged out þere,
Long sythen fro þe sounder þat siȝed for olde,
For he watȝ breme, bor alþer-grattest,
Ful grymme quen he gronyed; þenne greued mony,
For þre at þe fyrst þrast he þryȝt to þe erþe,
And sparred forth good sped boute spyt more.
Þise oþer halowed 'hyghe!' ful hyȝe, and 'hay! hay!' cryed,
Haden horneȝ to mouþe, heterly rechated;
Mony watȝ þe myry mouthe of men and of houndeȝ
þat buskkeȝ after þis bor with bost and wyth noyse
to quelle.
Ful oft he bydeȝ þe baye,
And maymeȝ þe mute inn melle;
He hurteȝ of þe houndeȝ, and þay
Ful ȝomerly ȝaule and ȝelle.

Schalkeȝ to schote at hym schowen to þenne,
Haled to hym of her areweȝ, hitten hym oft;
Bot þe poynteȝ payred at þe pyth þat pyȝt in his scheldeȝ,
And þe barbeȝ of his browe bite non wolde—
Þaȝ þe schauen schaft schyndered in peceȝ,
Þe hede hypped aȝayn were-so-euer hit hitte.
Bot quen þe dynteȝ hym dered of her dryȝe strokeȝ,
Þen, braynwod for bate, on burneȝ he raseȝ,
Hurteȝ hem ful heterly þer he forth hyȝeȝ,
And mony arȝed þerat, and on lyte droȝen.
Bot þe lorde on a lyȝt horce launces hym after,
As burne bolde vpon bent his bugle he bloweȝ;
He rechated, and rode þurȝ roneȝ ful þyk,
Suande þis wylde swyn til þe sunne schafted.
Þis day wyth þis ilk dede þay dryuen on þis wyse,

1440 fro: MS for siȝed: MS wiȝt
1441 breme *blotted and illegible*

down in rough confusion, they proceeded to the find, and the men followed them. The hunters cast about both the crag and the thicket, until they were quite sure that they had within their ring the beast whose presence had been announced by the bloodhounds. Then they beat the bushes, and called on him to rouse out, and he tried to escape through the line of men, with terrible effect; there rushed out a most magnificent boar, long since separated from the herd by age, for he was fierce, the biggest of boars, terrifying when he grunted; then many men were dismayed, for at the first rush he hurled three of them to the ground, and charged off at great speed, without doing any more harm. The others loudly shouted 'hi!', and cried 'hey! hey!', put their horns to their lips, vigorously sounding the rally; there was much merry din of men and hounds rushing after the boar with outcry and clamour to kill him. Repeatedly turning at bay, he tore at the pack all about him; he wounded some of the hounds, and they howled and yelped piteously.

Then men pressed forward to shoot at him, loosed their arrows at him, hitting him repeatedly; but the points which struck the hide on his shoulders were blunted by its toughness, and the barbs would not pierce his brow—though the smooth shaft was splintered to pieces, the head rebounded wherever it struck. But when the impact of their incessant blows hurt him, then, maddened by their baiting, he charged at the men, wounding them most savagely as he burst out, and at that many were afraid and drew back. But the lord on a swift horse dashed after him, blowing his bugle like a bold huntsman; he sounded the rally, and rode through the thick brushwood, pursuing the wild boar until the sun declined. So they passed the day in this pursuit, while our

Whyle oure luflych lede lys in his bedde,
Gawayn grayþely at home, in gereȝ ful ryche
of hewe.
Þe lady noȝt forȝate
To com hym to salue;
Ful erly ho watȝ hym ate
His mode for to remwe.

Ho commes to þe cortyn and at þe knyȝt totes.
Sir Wawen her welcumed worþy on fyrst,
And ho hym ȝeldeȝ aȝayn ful ȝerne of hir wordeȝ,
Setteȝ hir softly by his syde, and swyþely ho laȝeȝ,
And wyth a luflych loke ho layde hym þyse wordeȝ:
'Sir, ȝif ȝe be Wawen, wonder me þynkkeȝ,
Wyȝe þat is so wel wrast alway to god,
And conneȝ not of compaynye þe costeȝ vndertake,
And if mon kennes yow hom to knowe, ȝe kest hom of your mynde;
Þou hatȝ forȝeten ȝederly þat ȝisterday I taȝt te
Bi alder-truest token of talk þat I cowþe.'
'What is þat?' quoþ þe wyghe. 'Iwysse I wot neuer;
If hit be sothe þat ȝe breue, þe blame is myn awen.'
'Ȝet I kende yow of kyssyng,' quoþ þe clere þenne,
'Quere-so countenaunce is couþe quikly to clayme;
Þat bicumes vche a knyȝt þat cortaysy vses.'
'Do way,' quoþ þat derf mon, 'my dere, þat speche,
For þat durst I not do, lest I deuayed were;
If I were werned, I were wrang, iwysse, ȝif I profered.'
'Ma fay,' quoþ þe meré wyf, 'ȝe may not be werned;
Ȝe ar stif innoghe to constrayne wyth strenkþe, ȝif yow lykeȝ,
Ȝif any were so vilanous þat yow devaye wolde.'
'Ȝe, be God,' quoþ Gawayn, 'good is your speche,
Bot þrete is vnþryuande in þede þer I lende,
And vche gift þat is geuen not with goud wylle.
I am at your comaundement, to kysse quen yow lykeȝ;
Ȝe may lach quen yow lyst, and leue quen yow þynkkeȝ,
in space.'
Þe lady louteȝ adoun
And comlyly kysses his face;
Much speche þay þer expoun
Of druryes greme and grace.

1473 To com: MS Com to

fair knight lay in his bed, Gawain lay comfortably at home, under richly coloured coverlets. The lady did not neglect to come to wish him good morning; she was with him very early to get him to change his attitude.

Coming to the curtain of the bed, she peeped at the knight. Sir Gawain at once courteously welcomed her, and she very readily returned his greeting with her own, seating herself gently by his side and laughing freely, and with a loving glance she addressed these words to him: 'Sir, if you are really Gawain, it seems very strange to me that a knight who is so well disposed in every respect to noble behaviour, cannot comprehend the usages of polite society, and if someone instructs you in them, you put them out of your mind; you have promptly forgotten what I taught you yesterday in the very plainest words of instruction I could use.' 'What was that?' said the knight. 'I really have no idea; if what you say is true, the fault is wholly mine.' 'And yet I taught you about kissing,' replied the fair lady, 'where a lady's favour is manifest to claim it at once; it befits every knight who practises chivalry so to do.' 'Do not say such things, dear lady,' said the bold man, 'for that I dare not do, lest I should be denied; if I were refused, I would indeed be at fault for having made an advance.' 'Upon my word,' said the fair lady, 'no one could refuse you; you are strong enough to compel by force, if you choose, anyone who should be so ill-bred as to deny you.' 'Yes, truly,' said Gawain, 'what you say is correct, but the use of force is thought improper in the land where I live, and taking any gift that is not given with a good will. I am at your disposal, to kiss when you desire; you may begin when you wish, and leave off as soon as you think fit.' Bending down, the lady kissed his cheek with propriety; then they had much discourse concerning the pains and pleasures of love.

'I woled wyt at yow, wyȝe,' þat worþy þer sayde,
'And yow wrathed not þerwyth, what were þe skylle
Þat so ȝong and so ȝepe as ȝe at þis tyme,
So cortayse, so knyȝtyly, as ȝe ar knowen oute—
And of alle cheualry to chose, þe chef þyng alosed
Is þe lel layk of luf, þe lettrure of armes;
For to telle of þis teuelyng of þis trwe knyȝteȝ,
Hit is þe tytelet token and tyxt of her werkkeȝ,
How ledes for her lele luf hor lyueȝ han auntered,
Endured for her drury dulful stoundeȝ,
And after wenged with her walour and voyded her care,
And broȝt blysse into boure with bountees hor awen—
And ȝe ar knyȝt comlokest kyd of your elde,
Your worde and your worchip walkeȝ ayquere,
And I haf seten by yourself here sere twyes,
Ȝet herde I neuer of your hed helde no wordeȝ
Þat euer longed to luf, lasse ne more.
And ȝe, þat ar so cortays and coynt of your hetes,
Oghe to a ȝonke þynk ȝern to schewe
And teche sum tokeneȝ of trweluf craftes.
Why! ar ȝe lewed, þat alle þe los weldeȝ,
Oþer elles ȝe demen me to dille your dalyaunce to herken?
For schame!
I com hider sengel and sitte
To lerne at yow sum game;
Dos techeȝ me of your wytte,
Whil my lorde is fro hame.'

'In goud fayþe,' quoþ Gawayn, 'God yow forȝelde!
Gret is þe gode gle, and gomen to me huge,
Þat so worþy as ȝe wolde wynne hidere,
And pyne yow with so pouer a mon, as play wyth your knyȝt
With anyskynneȝ countenaunce; hit keuereȝ me ese.
Bot to take þe toruayle to myself to trwluf expoun,
And towche þe temeȝ of tyxt and taleȝ of armeȝ
To yow þat, I wot wel, weldeȝ more slyȝt
Of þat art, bi þe half, or a hundreth of seche
As I am, oþer euer schal, in erde þer I leue,
Hit were a folé felefolde, my fre, by my trawþe.
I wolde yowre wylnyng worche at my myȝt,

'I have wanted to learn from you, sir,' the noble lady then said, 'if it would not annoy you, what might be the reason that one so young and so valiant as you now are, so courteous, so chivalrous, as you are acknowledged far and wide to be—and in all the records of chivalric conduct, the thing most praised is the faithful practice of love, the gospel of the knightly profession; for, in describing the deeds of true knights, the inscribed title and text of these works is how men have ventured their lives for their true love, and for their love's sake endured grievous times, and have later vindicated themselves by their valour and put an end to their suffering, and brought happiness to their lady's bower by their own good qualities—and you are reputed the noblest knight of your generation, your fame and your honour are spread abroad everywhere, and I have sat beside you here on two separate occasions, yet I have never heard pass your lips any words that had anything to do with love, not one. And you, who are so courteous and polite in your assurances of knightly service, ought to offer readily to teach a young person some lessons in the arts of true love. What! are you, who enjoy such a reputation, so ignorant, or is it that you consider me too stupid to appreciate your courtly conversation? Shame on you! I have come here all alone and am sitting here to learn from you some amorous accomplishment; do teach me some of your love-lore, while my husband is away from home.'

'Upon my faith,' said Gawain, 'may God reward you! It is a great joy, an immense pleasure to me, that someone so noble as you should come here and trouble yourself with such a humble person, diverting yourself with your knight by showing him every kind of favour; it affords me delight. But to take upon myself the difficult task of expounding true love, and discoursing on the themes of romance and tales of chivalry to you, who, I know well, have more skill in that art, by far, than a hundred such as I am, or ever shall be, as long as I live on this earth, that would be a manifold folly, my noble lady, upon my word it would. I would wish to do what you desire as far as I can, since I am,

As I am hyȝly bihalden, and euermore wylle
Be seruaunt to yourseluen, so saue me Dryȝtyn!'
Þus hym frayned þat fre, and fondet hym ofte,
For to haf wonnen hym to woȝe, what-so scho þoȝt elleȝ;
Bot he defended hym so fayr þat no faut semed,
Ne non euel on nawþer halue, nawþer þay wysten
        bot blysse.
    Þay laȝed and layked longe;
    At þe last scho con hym kysse,
    Hir leue fayre con scho fonge,
    And went hir waye, iwysse.

Then ruþes hym þe renk and ryses to þe masse,
And siþen hor diner watȝ dyȝt and derely serued.
Þe lede with þe ladyeȝ layked alle day,
Bot þe lorde ouer þe londeȝ launced ful ofte,
Sweȝ his vncely swyn, þat swyngeȝ bi þe bonkkeȝ
And bote þe best of his bracheȝ þe bakkeȝ in sunder
Þer he bode in his bay, tel bawemen hit breken,
And madee hym mawgref his hed forto mwe vtter,
So felle floneȝ þer flete when þe folk gedered.
Bot ȝet þe styffest to start bi stoundeȝ he made,
Til at þe last he watȝ so mat he myȝt no more renne,
Bot in þe hast þat he myȝt he to a hole wynneȝ
Of a rasse bi a rokk þer renneȝ þe boerne.
He gete þe bonk at his bak, bigyneȝ to scrape,
Þe froþe femed at his mouth vnfayre bi þe wykeȝ,
Whetteȝ his whyte tuscheȝ. With hym þen irked
Alle þe burneȝ so bolde þat hym by stoden
To nye hym on-ferum, bot neȝe hym non durst
        for woþe.
    He hade hurt so mony byforne
    Þat al þuȝt þenne ful loþe
    Be more wyth his tuscheȝ torne,
    Þat breme watȝ and braynwod bothe,

Til þe knyȝt com hymself, kachande his blonk,
Syȝ hym byde at þe bay, his burneȝ bysyde.
He lyȝtes luflych adoun, leueȝ his corsour,

1580 and *supplied*

and always will be, deeply bound to be your faithful servant, so help me God!' In this way that noble lady tested him and tempted him repeatedly, in order to bring him to grief, whatever else she may have intended; but he defended himself so skilfully that no offence was apparent, nor any impropriety on either side, nor were they conscious of anything but contentment. They laughed and amused themselves for a long time; in the end she kissed him, courteously took her leave and, finally, departed.

Then the knight bestirred himself and rose to go to Mass, and then their dinner was prepared and splendidly served. The knight disported himself with the ladies all day, but the lord was constantly galloping across the country, pursuing his ferocious boar, which rushed over the hills and bit in two the backs of his best hounds wherever he stood at bay, till the bowmen broke his stand, and made him move into the open despite all he could do, so many arrows flew there when the hunt assembled. But nevertheless he made the bravest of them flinch at times, till at last he was so exhausted he could run no more, but with what speed he could he gained a hollow in a sheer cliff beside a boulder where the stream flowed by. He got the hillside at his back, and began to paw the ground, the froth foaming from the corners of his ugly mouth, as he whetted his white tusks. By now all the bold men who stood around him were weary of him, of harassing him from a distance, but none dared go near him because of the danger. He had injured so many already that now everyone felt very loath to be further torn by his tusks, fierce and frenzied as he was,

until the knight himself came up, urging on his mount, and saw him standing at bay, his followers surrounding him. Dismounting agilely

Braydeʒ out a bryʒt bront and bigly forth strydeʒ,
Foundeʒ fast þurʒ þe forth þer þe felle bydeʒ.
Þe wylde watʒ war of þe wyʒe with weppen in honde,
Hef hyʒly þe here, so hetterly he fnast
Þat fele ferde for þe freke, lest felle hym þe worre.
Þe swyn setteʒ hym out on þe segge euen,
Þat þe burne and þe bor were boþe vpon hepeʒ
In þe wyʒtest of þe water; þe worre hade þat oþer,
For þe mon merkkeʒ hym wel, as þay mette fyrst,
Set sadly þe scharp in þe slot euen,
Hit hym vp to þe hult, þat þe hert schyndered,
And he ʒarrande hym ʒelde, and ʒedoun þe water
ful tyt.
A hundreth houndeʒ hym hent,
Þat bremely con hym bite,
Burneʒ him broʒt to bent,
And doggeʒ to dethe endite.

There watʒ blawyng of prys in mony breme horne,
Heʒe halowing on hiʒe with haþeleʒ þat myʒt;
Brachetes bayed þat best, as bidden þe maystereʒ,
Of þat chargeaunt chace þat were chef huntes.
Þenne a wyʒe þat watʒ wys vpon wodcrafteʒ
To vnlace þis bor lufly bigynneʒ.
Fyrst he hewes of his hed and on hiʒe setteʒ,
And syþen rendeʒ him al roghe bi þe rygge after,
Braydeʒ out þe boweles, brenneʒ hom on glede,
With bred blent þerwith his braches rewardeʒ.
Syþen he britneʒ out þe brawen in bryʒt brode cheldeʒ,
And hatʒ out þe hastletteʒ, as hiʒtly bisemeʒ;
And ʒet hem halcheʒ al hole þe halueʒ togeder,
And syþen on a stif stange stoutly hem henges.
Now with þis ilk swyn þay swengen to home;
Þe bores hed watʒ borne bifore þe burnes seluen
Þat him forferde in þe forþe þurʒ forse of his honde
so stronge.
Til he seʒ Sir Gawayne
In halle hym þoʒt ful longe;
He calde, and he com gayn
His feeʒ þer for to fonge.

and letting his horse go, he drew a bright sword and strode forward powerfully, rapidly hastening over the ford to where the fierce beast stood at bay. The animal caught sight of the man with sword in hand, his bristles stood erect, and he snorted so fiercely that many were afraid for the knight, lest he should get the worst of the fight. The boar rushed straight at the knight, so that man and beast fell in a heap in the swiftest part of the stream; the latter had the worst of it, for the man, aiming directly at him, at their first encounter, firmly planted the sharp blade right in his throat, drove it up to the hilt, so that it cleft the heart, and, snarling, he gave in, and was quickly swept downstream. A hundred hounds seized him, biting him fiercely, the men dragged him to the bank, and the dogs finished him off.

The kill was sounded on many a glorious horn, hunters proudly shouting as loudly as they could; the hounds bayed over the beast, at the command of the masters-of-game, who had been the chief huntsmen in that arduous chase. Then a man who was skilled in woodcraft began neatly to cut up the boar. First he hews off his head and sets it up on a stake, and then afterwards divides him roughly along the backbone, pulls out the entrails, broils them on red-hot embers, and rewards his hounds with these mixed with bread. Next he slices up the flesh in broad white slabs, taking out the offal, as is right and proper; and also fastens the two sides together intact, and then slings them proudly from a stout pole. Now they set off for home with this beast; the boar's head was carried before the lord himself who had dispatched him in the stream by the might of his strong hand. The time seemed to him long until he set eyes on Sir Gawain in the castle hall; he summoned him, and he at once came to receive his dues there.

Þe lorde ful lowde with lote and laȝter myry,
When he seȝe Sir Gawayn, with solace he spekeȝ.
Þe goude ladyeȝ were geten, and gedered þe meyny;
He scheweȝ hem þe scheldeȝ and schapes hem þe tale
Of þe largesse and þe lenþe, þe liþerneȝ alse
Of the were of þe wylde swyn in wod þer he fled.
Þat oþer knyȝt ful comly comended his dedeȝ,
And praysed hit as gret prys þat he proued hade,
For suche a brawne of a best, þe bolde burne sayde,
Ne such sydes of a swyn segh he neuer are.
Þenne hondeled þay þe hoge hed, þe hende mon hit praysed,
And let lodly þerat þe lorde for to here.
'Now, Gawayn,' quoþ þe godmon, 'þis gomen is your awen
Bi fyn forwarde and faste, faythely ȝe knowe.'
'Hit is sothe,' quoþ þe segge, 'and as siker trwe
Alle my get I schal you gif agayn, bi my trawþe.'
He hent þe haþel aboute þe halse and hendely hym kysses,
And eftersones of þe same he serued hym þere.
'Now ar we euen,' quoþ þe haþel, 'in þis euentide,
Of alle þe couenauntes þat we knyt, syþen I com hider,
bi lawe.'
Þe lorde sayde, 'Bi saynt Gile,
Ȝe ar þe best þat I knowe!
Ȝe ben ryche in a whyle,
Such chaffer and ȝe drowe.'

Þenne þay teldet tableȝ trestes alofte,
Kesten cloþeȝ vpon; clere lyȝt þenne
Wakned bi woȝeȝ, waxen torches;
Seggeȝ sette and serued in sale al aboute.
Much glam and gle glent vp þerinne
Aboute þe fyre vpon flet, and on fele wyse
At þe soper and after, mony aþel songeȝ,
As coundutes of Krystmasse and caroleȝ newe,
With alle þe manerly merþe þat mon may of telle,
And euer oure luflych knyȝt þe lady bisyde.
Such semblaunt to þat segge semly ho made,
Wyth stille stollen countenaunce, þat stalworth to plese,

1623 laȝter: MS laȝed
1639 hent *supplied*

The lord, with loud voice and merry laugh, when he saw Sir Gawain, spoke to him joyfully. The worthy ladies were fetched, and the household assembled; he showed them the sides of meat and gave an account of the great girth and length of the wild boar, and also the ferocity of his resistance in the wood where he took refuge. The other knight most courteously commended his exploits, and praised as outstanding the qualities which he had displayed, for a beast with such flesh on it, the bold knight said, or a boar with such flanks, he had never seen before. Then they handled the huge head, the courteous knight admired it, and expressed horror at it in order to honour the lord. 'Now, Gawain,' said his host, 'this quarry is yours according to the agreement, fully ratified and binding, as you are well aware.' 'That is true,' said the knight, 'and just as faithfully, upon my word, I shall give you all my winnings in exchange.' He clasped the lord round the neck and kissed him courteously, and then immediately served him again in the same way. 'Now,' said the knight, 'for this evening we are fairly quit of all the conditions which we have drawn up in due form since I arrived here.' The lord said, 'By St Giles, you are the best man I know! You will be rich presently, if you carry on such a trade.'

Then tables were set up on trestles, and covered with cloths; next bright lights, waxen torches, were kindled on the walls; servants laid and served supper throughout the hall. Great noise of revelry and merriment arose there round the fire on the hearth, and, at the supper and afterwards, there were many splendid songs of various kinds, such as Christmas carols and the latest dance-songs, and every polite amusement one could describe, and all the while our courteous knight was at the lady's side. Her behaviour to the knight was so complaisant, with looks of favour slyly stolen, to please that bold knight, that he was quite

Þat al forwondered watȝ þe wyȝe, and wroth with hymseluen,
Bot he nolde not for his nurture nurne hir aȝaynez,
Bot dalt with hir al in daynté, how-se-euer þe dede turned
towrast.
Quen þay hade played in halle
As longe as hor wylle hom last,
To chambre he con hym calle,
And to þe chemné þay past.

Ande þer þay dronken and dalten, and demed eft nwe
To norne on þe same note on Nwe Ȝereȝ euen;
Bot þe knyȝt craued leue to kayre on þe morn,
For hit watȝ neȝ at þe terme þat he to schulde.
Þe lorde hym letted of þat, to lenge hym resteyed,
And sayde, 'As I am trwe segge, I siker my trawþe
Þou schal cheue to þe grene chapel þy charres to make,
Leude, on Nw Ȝereȝ lyȝt, longe bifore pryme.
Forþy þow lye in þy loft and lach þyn ese,
And I schal hunt in þis holt and halde þe towcheȝ,
Chaunge wyth þe cheuisaunce, bi þat I charre hider;
For I haf fraysted þe twys and faythful I fynde þe.
Now "þrid tyme, þrowe best" þenk on þe morne;
Make we mery quyl we may and mynne vpon joye,
For þe lur may mon lach when-so mon lykeȝ.'
Þis watȝ grayþely graunted and Gawayn is lenged,
Bliþe broȝt watȝ hym drynk, and þay to bedde ȝeden
with liȝt.
Sir Gawayn lis and sleþes
Ful stille and softe al niȝt;
Þe lorde þat his crafteȝ kepes,
Ful erly he watȝ diȝt.

After messe a morsel he and his men token;
Miry watȝ þe mornyng, his mounture he askes.
Alle þe haþeles þat on horse schulde helden hym after
Were boun busked on hor blonkkeȝ bifore þe halle ȝateȝ.
Ferly fayre watȝ þe folde, for þe forst clenged;
In rede rudede vpon rak rises þe sunne,
And ful clere costeȝ þe clowdes of þe welkyn.
Hunteres vnhardeled bi a holt syde,

bewildered, and troubled at heart, but his good breeding prevented him from rebuffing her, and he behaved with complete courtesy towards her, no matter how this might be misconstrued. When they had amused themselves in the hall as long as they wished, the lord summoned Gawain to his private room, and they betook themselves to the fireplace there.

And there they drank and chatted, and again agreed to observe the same terms once more on New Year's Eve; but the knight begged leave to depart on the morrow, for the tryst to which he had to go was near. The lord dissuaded him from this, prevailed on him to stay, saying, 'As I am a true knight, I give my word you shall reach the Green Chapel, there to do your business, sir, in the dawn of the New Year, long before prime. So you lie in your room and take your ease, and I shall hunt in the wood and fulfil the terms of the agreement, and exchange winnings with you when I return here; for I have tested you twice and I find you trustworthy. Now, "Third time pays for all", remember that tomorrow; but let us make merry while we may and give our minds to pleasure, for a man can be sad whenever he wishes.' This was readily agreed and Gawain persuaded to stay, drink was promptly brought them, and they went to bed with torches. Sir Gawain lay and slept very soundly and peacefully all night; the lord, who followed his own pursuits, was up and doing very early.

After Mass he and his men took a hasty bite; the morning was fine and he called for his mount. All the men who were to follow him on horseback were ready mounted on their horses before the hall portals. The countryside was wonderfully beautiful, for the frost clung to the ground; the sun rose red against the drifting rack, and in full radiance sailed amidst the clouds in the heavens. Huntsmen unleashed the hounds at the edge of a coppice, the rocky slopes in the wood

Rocheres roungen bi rys for rurde of her hornes.
Summe fel in þe fute þer þe fox bade,
Traylez ofte a traueres bi traunt of her wyles.
A kenet kryes þerof, þe hunt on hym calles;
His felazes fallen hym to, þat fnasted ful þike,
Runnen forth in a rabel in his ryzt fare.
And he fyskez hem byfore; þay founden hym sone,
And quen þay seghe hym with syzt þay sued hym fast,
Wrezande hym ful weterly with a wroth noyse;
And he trantes and tornayeez þurz mony tene greue,
Hauilounez and herkenez bi heggez ful ofte.
At þe last bi a littel dich he lepez ouer a spenne,
Stelez out ful stilly bi a strothe rande,
Went haf wylt of þe wode with wylez fro þe houndes.
Þenne watz he went, er he wyst, to a wale tryster,
Þer þre þro at a þrich þrat hym at ones,
 al graye.
 He blenched azayn bilyue
 And stifly start on-stray,
 With alle þe wo on lyue
 To þe wod he went away.

Thenne watz hit list vpon lif to lyþen þe houndez,
When alle þe mute hade hym met, menged togeder.
Suche a sorze at þat syzt þay sette on his hede
As alle þe clamberande clyffes hade clatered on hepes.
Here he watz halawed when haþelez hym metten,
Loude he watz zayned with zarande speche;
Þer he watz þreted and ofte þef called,
And ay þe titleres at his tayl, þat tary he ne myzt;
Ofte he watz runnen at when he out rayked,
And ofte reled in azayn, so Reniarde watz wylé.
And ze he lad hem bi lagmon, þe lorde and his meyny,
On þis maner bi þe mountes quyle myd-ouer-vnder,
Whyle þe hende knyzt at home holsumly slepez
Withinne þe comly cortynes, on þe colde morne.
Bot þe lady, for luf, let not to sleþe,

1700 traueres: MS trayteres
1719 list vpon lif: MS lif vpon list

resounding with the sound of their horns. Some of the hounds hit on the scent where the fox was lurking, repeatedly casting from side to side in cunning practice of their wiles. A whippet gave tongue at the scent, the huntsmen called others to join him; his fellows rallied to him, panting hard, and rushed forward in a pack hard on his trail. And the fox scampered before them; they soon sighted him, and when they laid eyes on him they pursued him swiftly, denouncing him in no uncertain terms with a furious noise; and he dodged and doubled back through many a tangled thicket, constantly turning to listen at the hedges. In the end he leapt over a fence beside a little ditch, stole out very quietly at the edge of an overgrown marsh, thinking he had by his tricks escaped from the wood away from the hounds. Then, before he was aware of it, he came upon a well placed hunting-station, where three fierce greyhounds all at once attacked him in a rush. He quickly shrank back again and sprang off vigorously on a new track, making off into the wood with despair in his heart.

Then it was good indeed to hear the hounds, when the whole pack, united as one, had come upon him. At the sight of him they called down on his head such an imprecation as though all the clustering crags had come clattering down in heaps. Here he was hallooed at when the hunters came upon him, loudly greeted with snarling words; there he was reviled and called a thief repeatedly, and the hounds were always on his tail, that he dared not pause; time and again he was attacked when he made for the open, and repeatedly he doubled back again, so wily was Reynard. And so in this way he led them at his heels, the lord and his followers, among the mountains until mid-afternoon, while the noble knight, for the good of his health, lay sleeping within the fair curtains, on this cold morning. But the lady, for love's sake, did not

Ne þe purpose to payre þat pyȝt in hir hert,
Bos ros hir vp radly, rayked hir þeder
In a mery mantyle, mete to þe erþe,
Þat watȝ furred ful fyne with felleȝ wel pured,
No hwef goud on hir hede bot þe haȝer stones
Trased aboute hir tressour be twenty in clusteres;
Hir þryuen face and hir þrote þrowen al naked,
Hir brest bare bifore, and bihinde eke.
Ho comeȝ withinne þe chambre dore, and closes hit hir after,
Wayueȝ vp a wyndow, and on þe wyȝe calleȝ,
And radly þus rehayted hym with hir riche wordeȝ,
        with chere:
    'A! mon, how may þou slepe?
    Þis morning is so clere.'
    He watȝ in drowping depe,
    Bot þenne he con hir here.

In dreȝ droupyng of dreme draueled þat noble,
As mon þat watȝ in mornyng of mony þro þoȝtes,
How þat destiné schulde þat day dele hym his wyrde
At þe grene chapel, when he þe gome metes,
And bihoues his buffet abide withoute debate more.
Bot quen þat comly com he keuered his wyttes,
Swenges out of þe sweuenes and swareȝ with hast.
Þe lady luflych com, laȝande swete,
Felle ouer his fayre face and fetly hym kyssed;
He welcumeȝ hir worþily with a wale chere.
He seȝ hir so glorious and gayly atyred,
So fautles of hir fetures and of so fyne hewes,
Wiȝt wallande joye warmed his hert.
With smoþe smylyng and smolt þay smeten into merþe,
Þat al watȝ blis and bonchef þat breke hem bitwene,
        and wynne.
    Þay lanced wordes gode,
    Much wele þen watȝ þerinne;
    Gret perile bitwene hem stod,
    Nif Maré of hir knyȝt mynne.

1738 hwef: MS hweȝ
1752 dele hym *supplied*
1755 com *supplied*

allow herself to sleep, nor the purpose that was rooted in her heart to weaken, but arose early, made her way thither in a gay robe, reaching to the ground, which was splendidly lined with well trimmed furs, no proper coif on her head, only well cut jewels set here and there on her coiffure in clusters of twenty; her fair face and throat were laid quite bare, her breast and back as well were both exposed. She came in at the chamber door and closed it behind her, threw open a window, and called to the knight, and immediately, in pleasant words, began gaily to rally him thus: 'Oh! sir, how can you sleep? the morning is so bright.' He was deep in troubled sleep, but he heard her then.

Deep in a dreaming torpor the noble knight was muttering, like a man troubled by many oppressive thoughts, of how Destiny would deal out his fate to him on the day when he was to meet the man at the Green Chapel, and must endure a blow from him without any resistance. But when that lovely lady entered he came to his senses, starting out of his dreams, and answered hurriedly. The fair lady came towards him, laughing sweetly, bent low over his handsome face and kissed him gracefully; he welcomed her courteously with a pleasant demeanour. When he saw her so lovely and so gaily dressed, so flawless in her person and with so perfect a complexion, joy ardently welling up warmed his heart. With courteous and gentle smiles they at once fell into merry conversation, so everything that passed between them was joy and happiness and delight. They spoke fair words, and had much pleasure in so doing; there was great peril between them, should Mary not be mindful of her knight.

For þat prynces of pris depresed hym so þikke,
Nurned hym so neȝe þe þred, þat nede hym bihoued
Oþer lach þer hir luf, oþer lodly refuse.
He cared for his cortaysye, lest craþayn he were,
And more for his meschef ȝif he schulde make synne,
And be traytor to þat tolke þat þat telde aȝt.
'God schylde,' quoþ þe schalk, 'þat schal not befalle!'
With luf-laȝyng a lyt he layd hym bysyde
Alle þe specheȝ of specialté þat sprange of her mouthe.
Quoþ þat burde to þe burne, 'Blame ȝe disserue,
Ȝif ȝe luf not þat lyf þat ȝe lye nexte,
Bifore alle þe wyȝeȝ in þe worlde wounded in hert,
Bot if ȝe haf a lemman, a leuer, þat yow lykeȝ better,
And folden fayth to þat fre, festned so harde
Þat yow lausen ne lyst—and þat I leue nouþe.
And þat ȝe telle me þat now trwly I pray yow;
For alle þe lufeȝ vpon lyue layne not þe soþe
for gile.'
Þe knyȝt sayde, 'Be sayn Jon,'
And smeþely con he smyle,
'In fayth I welde riȝt non,
Ne non wil welde þe quile.'

'Þat is a worde,' quoþ þat wyȝt, 'þat worst is of alle;
Bot I am swared for soþe, þat sore me þinkkeȝ.
Kysse me now comly, and I schal cach heþen;
I may bot mourne vpon molde, as may þat much louyes.'
Sykande ho sweȝe doun and semly hym kyssed,
And siþen ho seueres hym fro, and says as ho stondes,
'Now, dere, at þis departyng, do me þis ese,
Gif me sumquat of þy gifte, þi gloue if hit were,
Þat I may mynne on þe, mon, my mournyng to lassen.'
'Now iwysse,' quoþ þat wyȝe, 'I wolde I hade here
Þe leuest þing for þy luf þat I in londe welde,
For ȝe haf deserued, for soþe, sellyly ofte
More rewarde bi resoun þen I reche myȝt.
Bot to dele yow for drurye þat dawed bot neked!—
Hit is not your honour to haf at þis tyme

1770 prynces: MS prynce
1799 if: MS of

For that noble princess pressed him so hard, urged him so near to the limit, that he must needs either accept her love there and then, or refuse offensively. He was concerned for his courtesy, lest he should behave like a boor, and even more for his plight if he should commit a sin, and be a traitor to the man who owned that castle. 'God forbid,' said the knight, 'that shall not happen!' With some good-natured laughter he parried all the words of fond affection which fell from her lips. Said the lady to the knight, 'You deserve to be blamed, if you do not love the person who is here close to you, of all human kind the most sorely stricken at heart, unless you have a sweetheart, someone dearer to you, who pleases you better, and have plighted your troth to that noble lady, pledged it so firmly that you do not wish to break it—and that is what I now believe. And I beg you now to tell me so frankly; for the love of God and all the saints do not conceal the truth deceitfully.' The knight said, 'By St John,' and he smiled gently, 'I have none whatsoever, upon my honour, nor do I intend to have one at present.'

'That,' said the lady, 'is worse than anything else you could say; but I am indeed answered, and very painful I find it. Now be so good as to kiss me, and I will go away; as a woman who is much in love, I can only mourn throughout life.' Sighing, she stooped down and kissed him graciously, and then she parted from him, saying as she stood up, 'Now, my dear, at this parting, give me this consolation, give me something as a gift from you, if it should be only your glove, that I may be reminded of you, sir, to ease my grief.' 'Now really,' said the knight, 'I wish for your sake I had here the dearest thing that I possess on earth, for, truly, you have rightly deserved a reward many times greater than I could offer. But to give you as a love token something that would be of but little worth!—it is not fitting for you on this occasion to have a

A gloue for a garysoun of Gawaynez giftez,
And I am here an erande in erdez vncouþe,
And haue no men wyth no malez with menskful þingez;
Þat mislykez me, ladé, for luf at þis tyme,
Iche tolke mon do as he is tan, tas to non ille
ne pine.'
'Nay, hende of hyȝe honours,'
Quoþ þat lufsum vnder lyne,
'Þaȝ I hade noȝt of yourez,
Ȝet schulde ȝe haue of myne.'

Ho raȝt hym a riche rynk of red golde werkez,
Wyth a starande ston stondande alofte,
Þat bere blusschande bemez as þe bryȝt sunne;
Wyt ȝe wel, hit watz worth wele ful hoge.
Bot þe renk hit renayed, and redyly he sayde,
'I wil no giftez, for Gode, my gay, at þis tyme;
I haf none yow to norne, ne noȝt wyl I take.'
Ho bede hit hym ful bysily, and he hir bode wernes,
And swere swyftely his sothe þat he hit sese nolde;
And ho soré þat he forsoke, and sayde þerafter,
'If ȝe renay my rynk, to ryche for hit semez,
Ȝe wolde not so hyȝly halden be to me,
I schal gif yow my girdel, þat gaynes yow lasse.'
Ho laȝt a lace lyȝtly þat leke vmbe hir sydez,
Knit vpon hir kyrtel vnder þe clere mantyle,
Gered hit watz with grene sylke and with golde schaped,
Noȝt bot arounde brayden, beten with fyngrez;
And þat ho bede to þe burne, and blyþely bisoȝt,
Þaȝ hit vnworþi were, þat he hit take wolde.
And he nay þat he nolde neghe in no wyse
Nauþer golde ne garysoun, er God hym grace sende
To acheue to þe chaunce þat he hade chosen þere.
'And þerfore, I pray yow, displese yow noȝt,
And lettez be your bisinesse, for I bayþe hit yow neuer
to graunte.
I am derely to yow biholde
Bicause of your sembelaunt,

1815 noȝt: MS oȝt
1825 swyftely: MS swyftel

glove for a keepsake, as a gift from Gawain, and I am here on a mission in regions unknown, and have no servants and no baggage with fine things; I regret it now, my lady, for your sake, but every man must act according to his circumstances, so do not take it amiss or be offended.' 'No, no, noble knight of high repute,' said that lovely lady, 'even if I should get nothing of yours, yet you shall have something of mine.'

She offered him a splendid ring wrought in red gold, with a blazing jewel set in it, which shed gleaming rays like the bright sun; it was worth a great fortune, you can be sure. But the knight refused it, and said at once, 'I swear I will take no gifts at present, my fair lady; I have none to offer you, nor will I accept anything.' She pressed it on him most persistently, and he, refusing her offer, instantly swore on his honour that he would not take it; and she was grieved that he refused it, and so said, 'If you refuse my ring because it seems too costly, and you do not wish to be so greatly beholden to me, I shall give you my girdle, it will be of less value to you.' Swiftly she took a belt which was wrapped about her waist, fastened over her gown under the bright mantle, made of green silk and trimmed with gold, embroidered at the edges only, adorned with pendants; and this she offered to the knight, and laughingly begged that, though it might be of little value, he would take it. And he said that he would not on any account touch either ornament or keepsake, before God should grant him grace to accomplish the adventure to which he was then dedicated. 'And so, I beg you, do not let it offend you, and cease your importunity, for I will never consent to grant you this. I am deeply in your debt because of

And euer in hot and colde
To be your trwe seruaunt.'

'Now forsake ȝe þis silke,' sayde þe burde þenne,
'For hit is symple in hitself? And so hit wel semeȝ:
Lo! so hit is littel, and lasse hit is worþy.
Bot who-so knew þe costes þat knit ar þerinne,
He wolde hit prayse at more prys, parauenture;
For quat gome so is gorde with þis grene lace,
While he hit hade hemely halched aboute,
Þer is no haþel vnder heuen tohewe hym þat myȝt,
For he myȝt not be slayn for slyȝt vpon erþe.'
Þen kest þe knyȝt, and hit come to his hert
Hit were a juel for þe jopardé þat hym iugged were:
When he acheued to þe chapel his chek for to fech,
Myȝt he haf slypped to be vnslayn, þe sleȝt were noble.
Þenne he þulged with hir þrepe and þoled hir to speke,
And ho bere on hym þe belt and bede hit hym swyþe—
And he granted, and hym gafe with a goud wylle—
And bisoȝt hym, for hir sake, disceuer hit neuer,
Bot to lelly layne fro hir lorde; þe leude hym acordeȝ
Þat neuer wyȝe schulde hit wyt, iwysse, bot þay twayne,
for noȝte.
He þonkked hir oft ful swyþe,
Ful þro with hert and þoȝt.
Bi þat on þrynne syþe
Ho hatȝ kyst þe knyȝt so toȝt.

Thenne lachcheȝ ho hir leue and leueȝ hym þere,
For more myrþe of þat mon moȝt ho not gete.
When ho watȝ gon, Sir Gawayn gereȝ hym sone,
Rises and riches hym in araye noble,
Lays vp þe luf-lace þe lady hym raȝt,
Hid hit ful holdely þer he hit eft fonde.
Syþen cheuely to þe chapel choses he þe waye,
Preuély aproched to a prest, and prayed hym þere
Þat he wolde lyste his lyf and lern hym better

1863 fro: MS for
1872 ho: MS he
1878 lyste: MS lyfte

your kindness, and bound ever to be your faithful servant through thick and thin.'

'Are you now refusing this piece of silk,' the lady then said, 'because it is of no great value in itself? And so indeed it appears to be: see! it is so small, and of even less value. But anyone who knew the qualities that are interwoven in it would esteem it of more worth, perhaps; for anyone who is girt with this green girdle, while he has it closely wrapped about him, there is no mortal man who could cut him down, for he could not be killed by any stratagem whatsoever.' Then the knight considered, and it occurred to him that it would be a godsend for the perilous adventure which was assigned him: if, when he came to the chapel to meet his doom, he managed to escape being slain, it would be an excellent device. Then he bore with her insistence and allowed her to speak on, and she pressed the belt upon him and offered it to him urgently—and he consented and surrendered very willingly—and she begged him, for her sake, never to reveal it, but loyally to keep it from her husband; the knight promised that, assuredly, no one should ever know it on any account, but the two of them. He thanked her readily and repeatedly, most earnestly with heart and soul. Thereupon she kissed the bold knight for the third time.

Then she took her leave and left him there, for she could get no more amusement out of the knight. When she had gone, Sir Gawain quickly clothed himself, rising and dressing in splendid attire, and put away the love-lace the lady had given him, hiding it very carefully where he could find it later. Then first and foremost he betook himself to the chapel, went quietly to a priest and begged him there and then to hear his confession and teach him how his soul might be saved when he

How his sawle schulde be saued when he schuld seye heþen.
Þere he schrof hym schyrly and schewed his mysdedeȝ,
Of þe more and þe mynne, and merci besecheȝ,
And of absolucioun he on þe segge calles;
And he asoyled hym surely and sette hym so clene
As domeȝday schulde haf ben diȝt on þe morn.
And syþen he mace hym as mery among þe fre ladyes,
With comlych caroles and alle kynnes ioye,
As neuer he did bot þat daye, to þe derk nyȝt,
with blys.
Vche mon hade daynté þare
Of hym, and sayde, 'Iwysse,
Þus myry he watȝ neuer are,
Syn he com hider, er þis.'

Now hym lenge in þat lee, þer luf hym bityde!
Ȝet is þe lorde on þe launde ledande his gomnes.
He hatȝ forfaren þis fox þat he folȝed longe;
As he sprent ouer a spenne to spye þe schrewe,
Þer as he herd þe howndes þat hasted hym swyþe,
Renaud com richchande þurȝ a roȝe greue,
And alle þe rabel in a res ryȝt at his heleȝ.
Þe wyȝe watȝ war of þe wylde and warly abides,
And braydeȝ out þe bryȝt bronde and at þe best casteȝ.
And he schunt for þe scharp and schulde haf arered;
A rach rapes hym to, ryȝt er he myȝt,
And ryȝt bifore þe hors fete þay fel on hym alle,
And woried me þis wyly wyth a wroth noyse.
Þe lorde lyȝteȝ bilyue and lacheȝ hym sone,
Rased hym ful radly out of þe rach mouþes,
Haldeȝ heȝe ouer his hede, haloweȝ faste,
And þer bayen hym mony braþ houndeȝ.
Huntes hyȝed hem þeder with horneȝ ful mony,
Ay rechatande aryȝt til þay þe renk seȝen.
Bi þat watȝ comen his compeyny noble,
Alle þat euer ber bugle blowed at ones,
And alle þise oþer halowed þat hade no hornes;
Hit watȝ þe myriest mute þat euer men herde,

1906 lacheȝ: MS cacheȝ   hym: MS by
1909 braþ: MS bray

should pass away. Then he confessed himself fully and laid bare his sins, both big and small, imploring forgiveness, and begging the priest for absolution; and he absolved him fully and made him as pure as if Judgement Day were to fall upon the following day. And then the knight enjoyed himself with the noble ladies, with pleasant merry-making and every kind of delight, more than he had done on any other day, with great happiness, till nightfall. Everyone there delighted in his company and said, 'Indeed, he has never before been in such high spirits, since he came here.'

Now let us leave him there in comfort, and may love come his way! The lord is still in the field leading his men. He has headed off the fox which he has so long pursued; as he leapt over a hedge to get a sight of the rascal, hearing the hounds in hot pursuit, Reynard came making his way through a tangled thicket, and the whole pack in a rush right on his heels. The knight caught sight of the beast and, pausing cautiously and drawing out his bright sword, struck at the animal. And he flinched from the sharp blade and would have drawn back, but a hound rushed at him, before he could do so, and right in front of the horse's feet they all fell on him, and worried the wily beast with a fierce clamour. The lord, immediately dismounting and seizing him quickly, promptly snatched him out of the mouths of the dogs, held him high above his head, hallooing loudly, and many fierce hounds bayed at him. Huntsmen hurried up with many horns, continually sounding the rally in proper form until they came in sight of their lord. When his noble band had assembled, all who carried bugles blew them together, and all the rest who had no horns hallooed; it was the merriest cry that

Þe rich rurd þat þer watȝ raysed for Renaude saule
with lote.
Hor houndeȝ þay þer rewarde,
Her hedeȝ þay fawne and frote,
And syþen þay tan Reynarde
And tyruen of his cote.

And þenne þay helden to home, for hit watȝ nieȝ nyȝt,
Strakande ful stoutly in hor store horneȝ.
Þe lorde is lyȝt at þe laste at hys lef home,
Fyndeȝ fire vpon flet, þe freke þer-byside,
Sir Gawayn þe gode, þat glad watȝ withalle,
Among þe ladies for luf he ladde much ioye.
He were a bleaunt of blwe þat bradde to þe erþe;
His surkot semed hym wel þat softe watȝ forred,
And his hode of þat ilke henged on his schulder,
Blande al of blaunner were boþe al aboute.
He meteȝ me þis godmon inmyddeȝ þe flore,
And al with gomen he hym gret, and goudly he sayde,
'I schal fylle vpon fyrst oure forwardeȝ nouþe,
Þat we spedly han spoken þer spared watȝ no drynk.'
Þen acoles he þe knyȝt and kysses hym þryes,
As sauerly and sadly as he hem sette couþe.
'Bi Kryst,' quoþ þat oþer knyȝt, 'ȝe cach much sele
In cheuisaunce of þis chaffer, ȝif ȝe hade goud chepeȝ.'
'Ȝe, of þe chepe no charg,' quoþ chefly þat oþer,
'As is pertly payed þe porchaȝ þat I aȝte.'
'Mary,' quoþ þat oþer mon, 'myn is bihynde,
For I haf hunted al þis day, and noȝt haf I geten
Bot þis foule fox felle—þe fende haf þe godeȝ!—
And þat is ful pore for to pay for suche prys þinges
As ȝe haf þryȝt me here þro, suche þre cosses
so gode.'
'Inoȝ,' quoþ Sir Gawayn,
I þonk yow, bi þe rode,'
And how þe fox watȝ slayn
He tolde hym as þay stode.

1936 þe *supplied*
1941 porchaȝ: MS chepeȝ

ever was heard, the glorious uproar and clamour that was raised there for Reynard's soul. Then they rewarded their hounds, fondling and stroking their heads, and finally they took Reynard and stripped off his coat.

And then they made for home, for it was almost night, blowing vigorously on their powerful horns. At last the lord, having arrived at his pleasant home, found a fire upon the hearth, and the knight beside it, the good Sir Gawain who was entirely content, having experienced great pleasure from the friendship of the ladies. He was wearing a silken tunic of blue that reached to the ground; his surcoat, which was softly furred, suited him well, and his hood of the same material lay upon his shoulders, both of them trimmed all round with ermine. He met the master of the house in the middle of the hall, and greeted him very gaily, saying politely, 'This time I shall be the first to fulfil the terms of our compact, which we so fortunately agreed upon when the drink flowed freely.' Then he embraced the lord and gave him three kisses, with as much relish and vigour as he could deliver them. 'By Christ,' said the other knight, 'you are very fortunate to have obtained this merchandise, provided you struck good bargains.' 'Oh, never mind about the price,' said the other quickly, 'since I have openly paid over the goods that I obtained.' 'Marry,' said the other, 'mine is inferior, for I have hunted the whole of this day, and nothing have I gained but this miserable fox skin—the devil take such goods!—and that is a very poor return for such precious things as you have just now pressed on me so warmly, three such good kisses.' 'Say no more,' said Sir Gawain, 'by the rood, it is I who thank you,' and as they stood there the lord told him how the fox had been slain.

With merþe and mynstralsye, wyth meteȝ at hor wylle,
Þay maden as mery as any men moȝten—
With laȝyng of ladies, with loteȝ of bordes,
Gawayn and þe godemon so glad were þay boþe—
Bot if þe douthe had doted, oþer dronken ben oþer.
Boþe þe mon and þe meyny maden mony iapeȝ,
Til þe sesoun watȝ seȝen þat þay seuer moste;
Burneȝ to hor bedde behoued at þe laste.
Þenne loȝly his leue at þe lorde fyrst
Fochcheȝ þis fre mon, and fayre he hym þonkkeȝ:
'Of such a selly soiorne as I haf hade here,
Your honour at þis hyȝe fest, þe hyȝe kyng yow ȝelde!
I ȝef yow me for on of youreȝ, if yowreself lykeȝ,
For I mot nedes, as ȝe wot, meue to-morne,
And ȝe me take sum tolke to teche, as ȝe hyȝt,
Þe gate to þe grene chapel, as God wyl me suffer
To dele on Nw Ȝereȝ day þe dome of my wyrdes.'
'In god fayþe,' quoþ þe godmon, 'wyth a goud wylle
At þat euer I yow hyȝt halde schal I redé.'
Þer asyngnes he a seruaunt to sett hym in þe waye
And coundue hym by þe downeȝ, þat he no drechch had,
For to ferk þurȝ þe fryth and fare at þe gaynest
bi greue.
Þe lorde Gawayn con þonk,
Such worchip he wolde hym weue;
Þen at þo ladyeȝ wlonk
Þe knyȝt hatȝ tan his leue.

With care and wyth kyssyng he carppeȝ hem tille,
And fele þryuande þonkkeȝ he þrat hom to haue,
And þay ȝelden hym aȝayn ȝeply þat ilk;
Þay bikende hym to Kryst with ful colde sykyngeȝ.
Syþen fro þe meyny he menskly departes;
Vche mon þat he mette, he made hem a þonke
For his seruyse and his solace and his sere pyne
Þat þay wyth busynes had ben aboute hym to serue;
And vche segge as soré to seuer with hym þere
As þay hade wonde worþyly with þat wlonk euer.
Þen with ledes and lyȝt he watȝ ladde to his chambre

1962 selly: MS sellyly

With mirth and minstrelsy, with the dishes of their choice, they made as merry as any men could—with the laughter of the ladies, with jesting speeches, Gawain and the master of the house were both as happy as could be—unless the whole company had been demented, or else drunk. The lord and all his household too made many jokes, till the hour had come when they must separate; it was time at last for folks to go to their beds. First then the noble knight humbly took his leave of the lord, and thanked him courteously: 'For such a wonderful stay as I have had here, your hospitality at this high festival, may the Lord above reward you! I'll pledge you my services for those of one of your men, if it please you, for, as you know, I must needs be on my way tomorrow, if, as you promised, you will give me someone to show the way to the Green Chapel, there to receive on New Year's Day the fate my destiny holds in store.' 'Truly,' said the master of the house, 'all that ever I promised you I will readily fulfil, with a good will.' Then he assigned a servant to set him on the road and guide him over the hills, so that he would meet with no delay in riding through woodland and thicket by the shortest way. Gawain thanked the lord for showing him such consideration; then the knight took his leave of the noble ladies.

He spoke to them with regret, kissing them, and pressing upon them many hearty thanks, and they readily replied to him in the same manner; with grievous sighs they commended him to Christ. Next he courteously took leave of the household; to each man he spoke to, he gave thanks for his service and his kindness and for the particular trouble they had each taken to serve him diligently; and everyone was as sorry to part company with him there as if that noble knight had always lived in honour amongst them. Then, accompanied by men with lights, he was conducted to his chamber and brought contentedly

And blyþely broȝt to his bedde to be at his rest.
Ȝif he ne slepe soundyly say ne dar I,
For he hade muche on þe morn to mynne, ȝif he wolde,
in þoȝt.
Let hym lyȝe þere stille,
He hatȝ nere þat he soȝt;
And ȝe wyl a whyle be stylle,
I schal telle yow how þay wroȝt.

IV

Now neȝeȝ þe Nw Ȝere and þe nyȝt passeȝ,
Þe day dryueȝ to þe derk, as Dryȝtyn biddeȝ.
Bot wylde wedereȝ of þe worlde wakned þeroute,
Clowdes kesten kenly þe colde to þe erþe,
Wyth nyȝe innoghe of þe norþe, þe naked to tene;
Þe snawe snitered ful snart, þat snayped þe wylde;
Þe werbelande wynde wapped fro þe hyȝe,
And drof vche dale ful of dryftes ful grete.
Þe leude lystened ful wel, þat leȝ in his bedde,
Þaȝ he lowkeȝ his liddeȝ, ful lyttel he slepes;
Bi vch kok þat crue he knwe wel þe steuen.
Deliuerly he dressed vp er þe day sprenged,
For þere watȝ lyȝt of a laumpe þat lemed in his chambre.
He called to his chamberlayn, þat cofly hym swared,
And bede hym bryng hym his bruny and his blonk sadel;
Þat oþer ferkeȝ hym vp and fecheȝ hym his wedeȝ,
And grayþeȝ me Sir Gawayn vpon a grett wyse.
Fyrst he clad hym in his cloþeȝ, þe colde for to were,
And syþen his oþer harnays, þat holdely watȝ keped,
Boþe his paunce and his plateȝ, piked ful clene,
Þe ryngeȝ rokked of þe roust of his riche bruny;
And al watȝ fresch as vpon fyrst, and he watȝ fayn þenne
to þonk.
He hade vpon vche pece,
Wypped ful wel and wlonk;
Þe gayest into Grece,
Þe burne bede bryng his blonk.

to his bed to take his rest. Whether or not he slept soundly I should not like to say, for he had much to reflect upon in his thoughts concerning the morrow, if he cared to. Let him lie there undisturbed, for what he has been seeking is close at hand; if you will be silent for a little longer I shall tell you what occurred.

IV

Now the New Year was drawing near and the night passing, the dawn driving away the darkness, as the Lord commands. But outside wild winter storms arose, clouds drove the cold keenly down to the earth, with a bitter wind from the north, tormenting to those ill clad; the snow sleeted down bitingly, cruelly stinging the wild creatures; the whistling wind whipped down from the heights, and filled every valley full of great drifts. The knight as he lay in his bed listened intently, sleeping little, though he kept his eyelids closed; by every cock that crowed he was well aware the appointed day had come. He arose readily before the day dawned, for there was light from a lamp which shone in his room. He called to his body-servant, who answered him at once, and bade him bring his coat of mail and saddle his horse; the servant got up and brought him his apparel, and arrayed Sir Gawain in splendid fashion. First he dressed him in his clothes, to keep out the cold, and then in his other equipment, which had been carefully cared for, both his body armour and other pieces of plate, very brightly polished, the rings of his splendid coat of mail scoured free of rust; and it was all as clean as when new, and he then gladly gave thanks for that. He put on each fine, well polished piece; the handsomest knight in all the world ordered the man to bring his horse.

Whyle þe wlonkest wede he warp on hymseluen—
His cote wyth þe conysaunce of þe clere werkeȝ
Ennurned vpon veluet, vertuus stoneȝ
Aboute beten and bounden, enbrauded semeȝ,
And fayre furred withinne wyth fayre pelures—
Ȝet laft he not þe lace, þe ladieȝ gifte;
Þat forgat not Gawayn, for gode of hymseluen.
Bi he hade belted þe bronde vpon his balȝe hauncheȝ,
Þenn dressed he his drurye double hym aboute;
Swyþe sweþled vmbe his swange swetely þat knyȝt
Þe gordel of þe grene silke, þat gay wel bisemed,
Vpon þat ryol red cloþe þat ryche watȝ to schewe.
Bot wered not þis ilk wyȝe for wele þis gordel,
For pryde of þe pendaunteȝ, þaȝ polyst þay were,
And þaȝ þe glyterande golde glent vpon endeȝ,
Bot for to sauen hymself, when suffer hym byhoued
To byde bale withoute dabate of bronde hym to were
            oþer knyffe.
      Bi þat þe bolde mon boun
      Wynneȝ þeroute bilyue,
      Alle þe meyny of renoun
      He þonkkeȝ ofte ful ryue.

Thenne watȝ Gryngolet grayþe, þat gret watȝ and huge,
And hade ben soiourned sauerly and in a siker wyse;
Hym lyst prik for poynt, þat proude hors þenne.
Þe wyȝe wynneȝ hym to and wyteȝ on his lyre,
And sayde soberly hymself and by his soth swereȝ:
'Here is a meyny in þis mote þat on menske þenkkeȝ—
Þe mon hem maynteines, ioy mot þay haue;
Þe leue lady on lyue luf hir bityde.
Ȝif þay for charyté cherysen a gest,
And halden honour in her honde, þe haþel hem ȝelde
Þat haldeȝ þe heuen vpon hyȝe, and also yow alle!
And ȝif I myȝt lyf vpon londe lede any quyle,
I schuld rech yow sum rewarde redyly, if I myȝt.'
Þenn steppeȝ he into stirop and strydeȝ alofte;
His schalk schewed hym his schelde, on schulder he hit laȝt,
Gordeȝ to Gryngolet with his gilt heleȝ,

2025 wede: MS wedes

While he was putting on his noblest garment—his surcoat with the bright embroidered badge emblazoned upon velvet, set about and adorned with potent gems, embroidered at the seams, and finely furred inside with good pelts—he nevertheless did not omit the belt, the lady's gift; for his own good, Gawain did not forget that. When he had belted the sword about his sleek flanks, then he wound his love token around him twice; quickly and neatly the knight wrapped about his waist the girdle of green silk, which well suited that handsome figure, and looked splendid upon the royal scarlet cloth of the surcoat. But the knight did not wear the girdle for its richness, from pride in the pendants, polished though they were, and though gleaming gold glittered on its ends, but to protect himself, when he had to submit to facing death without resisting or defending himself with sword or dagger. When the valiant man, fully equipped, at once went outside, he repeatedly and heartily thanked all the noble retainers.

Then Gryngolet, tall and broad-backed, was ready, having been snugly and securely stabled; the proud steed was now in good condition and eager for a gallop. The knight went up to him and inspected his coat, and said quietly to himself, swearing upon his honour: 'In this castle here is a body of retainers who are mindful of due courtesy—joy be to them and the man who maintains them; as for the dear lady, may love be hers all her life long. Whenever out of charity they entertain a guest, and dispense hospitality, may the Lord who rules the heavens above reward them, and all of you as well! And if I should survive for long on this earth, I will reward you freely, if I can.' Then he set foot in the stirrup and vaulted up; his servant offered him his shield, and taking it upon his shoulder, he touched Gryngolet with his gilded spurs, and he

And he startez on þe ston, stod he no lenger
to praunce.
His haþel on hors watz þenne,
Þat bere his spere and launce.
'Þis kastel to Kryst I kenne':
He gef hit ay god chaunce.

The brygge watz brayde doun, and þe brode ȝatez
Vnbarred and born open vpon boþe halue.
Þe burne blessed hym bilyue, and þe bredez þassed—
Prayses þe porter, bifore þe prynce kneled,
Gef hym God and goud day, þat Gawayn he saue—
And went on his way with his wyȝe one,
Þat schulde teche hym to tourne to þat tene place
Þer þe ruful race he shulde resayue.
Þay boȝen bi bonkkez þer boȝez ar bare,
Þay clomben bi clyffez þer clengez þe colde.
Þe heuen watz vphalt, bot vgly þervnder;
Mist muged on þe mor, malt on þe mountez,
Vch hille hade a hatte, a myst-hakel huge.
Brokez byled and breke bi bonkkez aboute,
Schyre schaterande on schorez, þer þay doun schowued.
Wela wylle watz þe way þer þay bi wod schulden,
Til hit watz sone sesoun þat þe sunne ryses
þat tyde.
Þay were on a hille ful hyȝe,
Þe quyte snaw lay bisyde;
Þe burne þat rod hym by
Bede his mayster abide.

'For I haf wonnen yow hider, wyȝe, at þis tyme,
And now nar ȝe not fer fro þat note place
Þat ȝe han spied and spuryed so specially after.
Bot I schal say yow for soþe, syþen I yow knowe,
And ȝe ar a lede vpon lyue þat I wel louy,
Wolde ȝe worch bi my wytte, ȝe worþed þe better.
Þe place þat ȝe prece to ful perelous is halden;
Þer wonez a wyȝe in þat waste, þe worst vpon erþe,
For he is stiffe and sturne, and to strike louies,
And more he is þen any mon vpon myddelerde,

stood prancing no longer, but leapt forward over the flagstones. His guide, who bore his spear and lance, was already mounted. 'This castle I commend to Christ,' said Gawain, wishing good fortune to it evermore.

The drawbridge was lowered and the wide gates unbarred and laid open on both sides. The knight crossed himself quickly, and passed over the planks—praising the porter who, on his knees before the prince, wished him good day and commended him to God, praying Him to preserve Gawain—and went on his way alone with his man, who was to guide him in going to that perilous place where he was to receive the grievous blow. They journeyed through hills where the boughs were bare, they climbed over cliffs to which the cold clung. The clouds were high, but lowering; mist drizzled over the moor, dissolved upon the mountain-tops, every hill wore a hat, a huge cape of mist. Brooks boiled and foamed on the hillsides round about, dashing white against their banks, where the riders made their way down. It was a very wandering way they had to follow through the forest, till soon the time came when the sun rises at that season of the year. They were high on a hill, where the white snow lay round about; the man who rode beside him bade his master halt.

'For, sir, I have now brought you thus far, and now you are not far from that notorious place which you have sought for and asked after so particularly. But, since I know you, and you are of all mortal men one whom I love well, I shall tell you frankly that, if you would do as I advise, it would be the better for you. The place which you are hastening towards is held to be very perilous; in that wasteland there lives a man, the most evil in the world, for he is bold and fierce, and loves to strike blows, and he is bigger than any man on this earth, and

And his body bigger þen þe best fowre
Þat ar in Arþurez hous, Hestor, oþer oþer.
He cheuez þat chaunce at þe chapel grene,
Þer passes non bi þat place so proude in his armes
Þat he ne dyngez hym to deþe with dynt of his honde;
For he is a mon methles, and mercy non vses,
For be hit chorle oþer chaplayn þat bi þe chapel rydes,
Monk oþer masseprest, oþer any mon elles,
Hym þynk as queme hym to quelle as quyk go hymseluen.
Forþy I say þe, as soþe as ʒe in sadel sitte,
Com ʒe þere, ʒe be kylled, may þe knyʒt rede,
Trawe ʒe me þat trwely, þaʒ ʒe had twenty lyues
to spende.
He hatʒ wonyd here ful ʒore,
On bent much baret bende;
Aʒayn his dyntez sore
Ʒe may not yow defende.

'Forþy, goude Sir Gawayn, let þe gome one,
And gotʒ away sum oþer gate, vpon Goddez halue!
Cayrez bi sum oþer kyth, þer Kryst mot yow spede,
And I schal hyʒ me hom aʒayn, and hete yow fyrre
Þat I schal swere bi God and alle his gode halʒez,
As help me God and þe halydam, and oþez innoghe,
Þat I schal lelly yow layne and lance neuer tale
Þat euer ʒe fondet to fle for freke þat I wyst.'
'Grant merci,' quoþ Gawayn, and gruchyng he sayde:
'Wel worth þe, wyʒe, þat woldez my gode,
And þat lelly me layne I leue wel þou woldez.
Bot helde þou hit neuer so holde, and I here passed,
Founded for ferde for to fle, in fourme þat þou tellez,
I were a knyʒt kowarde, I myʒt not be excused.
Bot I wyl to þe chapel, for chaunce þat may falle,
And talk wyth þat ilk tulk þe tale þat me lyste,
Worþe hit wele oþer wo, as þe wyrde lykez
hit hafe.
Þaʒe he be a sturn knape
To stiʒtel, and stad with staue,
Ful wel con Dryʒtyn schape
His seruauntez for to saue.'

stronger in body than the four best knights who are in Arthur's household, or Hector, or anyone else. He brings it about at the Green Chapel that no one passes by that place, however proud of his prowess in arms, whom he does not strike dead with a blow of his hand; for he is a ruthless man, and shows no mercy, for be it peasant or cleric who rides past the chapel, monk or priest, or any other man, he thinks it as pleasant to kill him as to be alive himself. And so I tell you, as surely as you sit there in the saddle, should you go there you will be killed, if the knight has his way, believe me, that is certain, though you had twenty lives to lose. He has lived here a very long while, causing much strife in the country; against his cruel blows you cannot defend yourself.

'Therefore, good Sir Gawain, let the man alone, and go away by some other path, for God's sake! Ride to some other land, where Christ may prosper you, and I will hurry home again, and I promise you, moreover, that I shall swear by God and all his good saints, so help me God and the holy relics, and many another oath, that I will keep your secret loyally and never utter a word that you ever ran away from any man that I knew of.' 'Many thanks,' said Gawain, and he added coldly: 'Good luck befall you, sir, who wish my good, and I am quite sure you would keep my secret loyally. But however faithfully you kept it, if I passed by this place, took to flight out of fear, in the way you suggest, I should be a cowardly knight, and there would be no excuse for me. But I mean to go to the chapel, no matter what may happen there, and have what talk I please with that man, whether the outcome be good or bad, as Fate will have it. Though he may be a grim fellow to deal with, and armed with a club, the Lord is well able to protect his servants.'

'Mary!' quoþ þat oþer mon, 'now þou so much spelleȝ
Þat þou wylt þyn awen nye nyme to þyseluen,
And þe lyst lese þy lyf, þe lette I ne kepe.
Haf here þi helme on þy hede, þi spere in þi honde,
And ryde me doun þis ilk rake bi ȝon rokke syde,
Til þou be broȝt to þe boþem of þe brem valay.
Þenne loke a littel on þe launde, on þi lyfte honde,
And þou schal se in þat slade þe self chapel,
And þe borelych burne on bent þat hit kepeȝ.
Now fareȝ wel, on Godeȝ half, Gawayn þe noble!
For alle þe golde vpon grounde I nolde go wyth þe,
Ne bere þe felaȝschip þurȝ þis fryth on fote fyrre.'
Bi þat þe wyȝe in þe wod wendeȝ his brydel,
Hit þe hors with þe heleȝ as harde as he myȝt,
Lepeȝ hym ouer þe launde, and leueȝ þe knyȝt þere
al one.
'Bi Goddeȝ self,' quoþ Gawayn,
'I wyl nauþer grete ne grone;
To Goddeȝ wylle I am ful bayn,
And to hym I haf me tone.'

Thenne gyrdeȝ he to Gryngolet and gedereȝ þe rake,
Schowueȝ in bi a schore at a schaȝe syde,
Rideȝ þurȝ þe roȝe bonk ryȝt to þe dale.
And þenne he wayted hym aboute, and wylde hit hym þoȝt,
And seȝe no syngne of resette bisydeȝ nowhere,
Bot hyȝe bonkkeȝ and brent vpon boþe halue,
And ruȝe knokled knarreȝ with knorned stoneȝ;
Þe skweȝ of þe scowtes skayned hym þoȝt.
Þenne he houed and wythhylde his hors at þat tyde,
And ofte chaunged his cher þe chapel to seche.
He seȝ non suche in no syde, and selly hym þoȝt,
Saue, a lyttel on a launde, a lawe as hit were,
A balȝ berȝ bi a bonke þe brymme bysyde,
Bi a forȝ of a flode þat ferked þare;
Þe borne blubred þerinne as hit boyled hade.
Þe knyȝt kacheȝ his caple and com to þe lawe,
Liȝteȝ doun luflyly, and at a lynde tacheȝ
Þe rayne and his riche with a roȝe braunche.
Þenne he boȝeȝ to þe berȝe, aboute hit he walkeȝ,

'Marry,' said the other man, 'now you go so far as to say that you wish to bring your own doom upon yourself, and if it pleases you to lose your life, I have no wish to hinder you. Here, put your helmet on your head, take your spear in your hand, and ride down this path here by the side of that rock, till it brings you to the bottom of this wild valley. Then look a little to your left, across the open ground, and you will see in the valley bottom that very chapel, and the huge warrior who guards it. Now farewell, in God's name, noble Gawain! Not for all the gold on earth would I go with you, or keep you company through this forest one foot further.' With that the man jerked his bridle round, there in the wood, struck his horse with the spurs as hard as he could, galloped across the glade, and left the knight there all alone. 'By God,' said Gawain, 'I will not weep or moan; I am wholly obedient to God's will, and have committed myself utterly to him.'

Then setting spurs to Gryngolet and picking up the path, he pressed onward, past a rock, at the edge of a thicket, and rode down the rugged slope right to the valley bottom. Then he looked about him, and a wild spot it seemed to him, and he saw no sign of habitation anywhere about, only steep and lofty hills on either hand, and rough, gnarled rocks with rugged outcrops; the jutting crags seemed to him to graze the clouds. Then, reining in his horse, he halted there, and repeatedly turned his gaze this way and that, to look for the chapel. He saw nothing of the kind in any direction, which seemed to him strange, except, at a short distance across a glade, what looked like a knoll, a rounded mound on the side of a slope by the water's edge, near the channel of a stream which flowed there; the burn seethed and foamed in its bed as though it were boiling. Urging on his horse, the knight came to the knoll, dismounted agilely, and fastened his noble steed by the reins to the rough branch of a linden tree. Then, going up to the mound, he walked round it, deliberating with himself as to what it

Debatande with hymself quat hit be myȝt.
Hit hade a hole on þe ende and on ayþer syde,
And ouergrowen with gresse in glodes aywhere,
And al watȝ holȝ inwith, nobot an olde caue,
Or a creuisse of an olde cragge—he couþe hit noȝt deme
with spelle.
'We! Lorde,' quoþ þe gentyle knyȝt,
'Wheþer þis be þe grene chapelle?
Here myȝt aboute mydnyȝt
Þe dele his matynnes telle!

'Now iwysse,' quoþ Wowayn, 'wysty is here;
Þis oritore is vgly, with erbeȝ ouergrowen;
Wel bisemeȝ þe wyȝe wruxled in grene
Dele here his deuocioun on þe deueleȝ wyse.
Now I fele hit is þe fende, in my fyue wytteȝ,
Þat hatȝ stoken me þis steuen to strye me here.
Þis is a chapel of meschaunce, þat chekke hit bytyde!
Hit is þe corsedest kyrk þat euer I com inne!'
With heȝe helme on his hede, his launce in his honde,
He romeȝ vp to þe roffe of þo roȝ woneȝ.
Þene herde he of þat hyȝe hil, in a harde roche
Biȝonde þe broke, in a bonk, a wonder breme noyse.
Quat! hit clatered in þe clyff as hit cleue schulde,
As one vpon a gryndelston hade grounden a syþe.
What! hit wharred and whette as water at a mulne;
What! hit rusched and ronge, rawþe to here.
Þenne 'Bi Godde,' quoþ Gawayn, 'þat gere, as I trowe,
Is ryched at þe reuerence me, renk, to mete
bi rote.
Let God worche! "We loo"—
Hit helppeȝ me not a mote.
My lif þaȝ I forgoo,
Drede dotȝ me no lote.'

Thenne þe knyȝt con calle ful hyȝe:
'Who stiȝtleȝ in þis sted, me steuen to holde?
For now is gode Gawayn goande ryȝt here.
If any wyȝe oȝt wyl, wynne hider fast,

2205 as: MS at

could be. It had a hole at one end and one at each side, and was all overgrown with patches of grass, and quite hollow inside, nothing but an old cave, or a fissure in an old crag—he could not say what it was. 'Ah! Lord,' said the noble knight, 'can this be the Green Chapel? The Devil might well recite his matins here about midnight!

'Now, truly,' said Gawain, 'this is a desolate place; this chapel, overgrown with weeds, is evil-looking; it is very fitting for the man clad in green to perform his devotions here according to the Devil's usage. Now I feel, in my whole being, that it is the Devil who has imposed this tryst on me in order to destroy me here. This is a chapel of doom, ill luck befall it! It is the most unhallowed church that ever I entered!' With his lofty helmet on his head, his lance in his hand, he made his way up to the roof of the rough dwelling. Then from that high mound he heard, within a solid rock on a slope beyond the brook, a wondrous loud noise. Hark! it re-echoed within the cliff as though it would split it, as if someone were sharpening a scythe upon a grindstone. Hark! it whirred and rasped like water at a mill; hark! it screeched and rang, horrible to hear. Then said Gawain, 'By God, this contrivance, I believe, is intended to honour me, to greet a knight with due ceremony. Let God's will be done! To cry "alas" will help me not one whit. Even though I lose my life, no noise shall make me afraid.'

Then the knight called out loudly: 'Who is master in this place, to keep tryst with me? For now Gawain, true to his word, is here, on this spot. If any man wants anything, let him come here quickly, now or never,

Oþer now oþer neuer, his nedeȝ to spede.'
'Abyde,' quoþ on on þe bonke abouen ouer his hede,
'And þou schal haf al in hast þat I þe hyȝt ones.'
Ȝet he rusched on þat rurde rapely a þrowe,
And wyth quettyng awharf, er he wolde lyȝt.
And syþen he keuereȝ bi a cragge and comeȝ of a hole,
Whyrlande out of a wro wyth a felle weppen,
A deneȝ ax nwe dyȝt, þe dynt with to ȝelde,
With a borelych bytte bende by þe halme,
Fyled in a fylor, fowre fote large—
Hit watȝ no lasse, bi þat lace þat lemed ful bryȝt.
And þe gome in þe grene gered as fyrst,
Boþe þe lyre and þe leggeȝ, lokkeȝ and berde,
Saue þat fayre on his fote he foundeȝ on þe erþe,
Sette þe stele to þe stone and stalked bysyde.
When he wan to þe watter, þer he wade nolde,
He hypped ouer on hys ax, and orpedly strydeȝ,
Bremly broþe on a bent þat brode watȝ aboute,
on snawe.
Sir Gawayn þe knyȝt con mete,
He ne lutte hym noþyng lowe;
Þat oþer sayde, 'Now, sir swete,
Of steuen mon may þe trowe.

'Gawayn,' quoþ þat grene gome, 'God þe mot loke!
Iwysse þou art welcom, wyȝe, to my place,
And þou hatȝ tymed þi trauayl as truee mon schulde,
And þou knoweȝ þe couenaunteȝ kest vus bytwene:
At þis tyme twelmonyth þou toke þat þe falled,
And I schulde at þis Nwe Ȝere ȝeþly þe quyte.
And we ar in þis valay verayly oure one;
Here ar no renkes vs to rydde, rele as vus likeȝ.
Haf þy helme of þy hede, and haf here þy pay;
Busk no more debate þen I þe bede þenne
When þou wypped of my hede at a wap one.'
'Nay, bi God,' quoþ Gawayn, 'þat me gost lante,
I schal gruch þe no grwe for grem þat falleȝ.
Bot styȝtel þe vpon on strok, and I schal stonde stylle
And warþ þe no wernyng to worch as þe lykeȝ,
nowhare.'

to dispatch his business.' 'Wait,' said someone up on the hillside above his head, 'and you shall quickly have all that I once promised you.' Still he went rapidly on with that whirring noise for a time, turning back to his grinding, before he would come down. And then he made his way down by the side of a crag and emerged from a fissure, came hurtling out of a cleft with a terrible weapon, a Danish axe freshly prepared, with which to return the blow, having a massive blade curving back upon the shaft, sharpened on a grindstone, and four feet in length—it was no less, measured against that belt, the brightly shining girdle. And, as before, the man was arrayed in green, face and legs as well, hair and beard, except that he now went afoot, striding firmly over the ground, planting the handle on the rock beside him as he stalked along. When he came to the stream, not wishing to wade it, he vaulted over on his axe, and strode vigorously, fierce and furious, over the broad stretch of snow that lay all round. Sir Gawain greeted the knight, but his bow was by no means a low one; the other said, 'So, good sir, you can be trusted to keep tryst.

'Gawain,' said the Green Knight, 'God keep you! you are truly welcome, sir, to my dwelling, and you have timed your journey as an honest man should, knowing the terms arranged between us: at this time twelve months ago you were to take what fell to your lot, and I was to repay you promptly on this New Year's Day. Now we are entirely on our own in this valley; there are no men here to part us, we can struggle as we please. Take your helmet from your head, and take what is due to you now; make no more resistance than I offered to you when you whipped off my head at a single blow.' 'No,' said Gawain, 'by God who gave me life, I shall not bear you the slightest grudge whatever harm befalls me. Only limit yourself to one stroke, and I will stand still and offer no resistance whatsoever to your doing as you

He lened with þe nek and lutte,
And schewed þat schyre al bare,
And lette as he noȝt dutte;
For drede he wolde not dare.

Then þe gome in þe grene grayþed hym swyþe,
Gedereȝ vp hys grymme tole, Gawayn to smyte;
With alle þe bur in his body he ber hit on lofte,
Munt as maȝtyly as marre hym he wolde.
Hade hit dryuen adoun as dreȝ as he atled,
Þer hade ben ded of his dynt þat doȝty watȝ euer.
Bot Gawayn on þat giserne glyfte hym bysyde,
As hit com glydande adoun on glode hym to schende,
And schranke a lytel with þe schulderes for þe scharp yrne.
Þat oþer schalk wyth a schunt þe schene wythhaldeȝ,
And þenne repreued he þe prynce with mony prowde wordeȝ:
'Þow art not Gawayn,' quoþ þe gome, 'þat is so goud halden,
Þat neuer arȝed for no here by hylle ne be vale,
And now þou fles for ferde er þou fele harmeȝ!
Such cowardise of þat knyȝt cowþe I neuer here.
Nawþer fyked I ne flaȝe, freke, quen þou myntest,
Ne kest no kauelacion in kyngeȝ hous Arthor.
My hede flaȝ to my fote, and ȝet flaȝ I neuer;
And þou, er any harme hent, arȝeȝ in hert.
Wherfore þe better burne me burde be called
þerfore.'
Quoþ Gawayn, 'I schunt oneȝ,
And so wyl I no more;
Bot þaȝ my hede falle on þe stoneȝ,
I con not hit restore.

'Bot busk, burne, bi þi fayth, and bryng me to þe poynt.
Dele to me my destiné and do hit out of honde,
For I schal stonde þe a strok, and start no more
Til þyn ax haue me hitte—haf here my trawþe.'
'Haf at þe þenne!' quoþ þat oþer, and heueȝ hit alofte,
And wayteȝ as wroþely as he wode were.
He mynteȝ at hym maȝtyly, bot not þe mon ryneȝ,
Withhelde heterly his honde er hit hurt myȝt.
Gawayn grayþely hit bydeȝ and glent with no membre,

please.' He bent his neck and bowed down, exposing the white skin all uncovered, and behaved as if he feared nothing; he would not tremble with terror.

Then the Green Knight got ready in an instant, lifting up his grim weapon to strike Gawain; with all the strength in his body he raised it aloft, swung it as powerfully as if he intended to destroy him. Had it come hurtling down as forcibly as he seemed to intend, then his blow would have killed that ever-valiant knight. But Gawain glanced sideways at the battle-axe, as it came gliding down earthwards to destroy him, and his shoulders shrank a little from the keen steel. The other man checked the bright blade with a sudden jerk, and then he rebuked the prince with many haughty words: 'You are not Gawain,' said the man, 'Gawain who is considered so good a knight, who never feared any power on earth, and now you are flinching for fear before you feel any injury! I never heard of such cowardice on the part of that knight. I neither flinched nor budged, sir, when you struck at me, nor made any objection in King Arthur's court. My head fell at my feet, and yet I did not flinch at all; and you, before you have received any injury, quail at heart. So therefore I ought to be acknowledged the better man.' Said Gawain, 'I flinched once, but I will do so no more; though if my head falls on the stones, I cannot restore it.

'But hurry up, man, for your honour's sake, and come to the point with me. Mete out my fate to me and do it out of hand, for I shall stand still and take a stroke from you, and flinch no more till your axe has struck me—take my word for it.' 'Have at you, then!' said the other, and raised the axe aloft, glaring as fiercely as though he were mad. He swung at him powerfully but, without touching the knight, checked his hand suddenly before it could do any harm. Gawain, steadfastly awaiting it, did not flinch in any limb, but stood still as a stone, or a tree

Bot stode stylle as þe ston, oþer a stubbe auþer
Þat raþeled is in roché grounde with rotez a hundreth.
Þen muryly efte con he mele, þe mon in þe grene:
'So, now þou hatz þi hert holle, hitte me bihous.
Halde þe now þe hyze hode þat Arþur þe razt,
And kepe þy kanel at þis kest, zif hit keuer may.'
Gawayn ful gryndelly with greme þenne sayde:
'Wy! þresch on, þou þro mon, þou þretez to longe;
I hope þat þi hert arze wyth þyn awen seluen.'
'For soþe,' quoþ þat oþer freke, 'so felly þou spekez,
I wyl no lenger on lyte lette þin ernde
        rizt nowe.'
    Þenne tas he hym stryþe to stryke,
    And frounsez boþe lyppe and browe;
    No meruayle þaz hym myslyke
    Þat hoped of no rescowe.

He lyftes lyztly his lome and let hit doun fayre
With þe barbe of þe bitte bi þe bare nek.
Þaz he homered heterly, hurt hym no more
Bot snyrt hym on þat on syde, þat seuered þe hyde.
Þe scharp schrank to þe flesche þurz þe schyre grece,
Þat þe schene blod ouer his schulderes schot to þe erþe.
And quen þe burne sez þe blode blenk on þe snawe,
He sprit forth spenne-fote more þen a spere lenþe,
Hent heterly his helme and on his hed cast,
Schot with his schulderez his fayre schelde vnder,
Braydez out a bryzt sworde, and bremely he spekez—
Neuer syn þat he watz burne borne of his moder,
Watz he neuer in þis worlde wyze half so blyþe—
'Blynne, burne, of þy bur, bede me no mo!
I haf a stroke in þis sted withoute stryf hent,
And if þow rechez me any mo, I redyly schal quyte,
And zelde zederly azayn—and þerto ze tryst—
        and foo.
    Bot on stroke here me fallez—
    Þe couenaunt schop ryzt so,
    Fermed in Arthurez hallez—
    And þerfore, hende, now hoo!'

2329 Fermed: MS ferl *remainder illegible*

stump that is anchored in rocky ground by a hundred roots. Then the man in green spoke again, playfully: 'So, now that you have regained your courage, I really must strike you. May the exalted order of knighthood which Arthur conferred on you preserve you now, and save your neck at this stroke, if it can.' Then Gawain, very angry, said furiously: 'Ah! strike away, you fierce fellow, you threaten too long; I believe you have struck fear into your own heart.' 'Faith,' said the other man, 'you speak so fiercely that I will no longer delay or defer your business further.' Then he took his stance for the blow, puckering lips and brow alike; no wonder Gawain, who had no hope of escape, blenched at it.

Lifting his weapon lightly, he let it down deftly with the edge of the blade just by the naked neck. Though he had struck fiercely, he did him no more injury than to graze him on one side, just breaking the skin. The sharp blade penetrated through the white fat into the flesh, so that the bright blood spurted over his bowed shoulders to the ground. And when the knight saw the blood gleaming on the snow, he sprang forward in a great leap more than a spear's length, quickly seized his helmet and put it on his head, with a movement of his shoulders jerked down his fine shield, drew out a bright sword, and spoke fiercely—never since his mother bore him had he ever been half so happy as then—'Cease your attack, sir, offer me no more blows! I have taken one blow in this place without resistance, and if you give any more, I will repay you readily, and return them promptly—be sure of that—and in earnest. Only one stroke is due me here—the agreement made in Arthur's court was so framed—and so, good sir, hold your hand!'

The haþel heldet hym fro and on his ax rested,
Sette þe schaft vpon schore and to þe scharp lened,
And loked to þe leude þat on þe launde ȝede,
How þat doȝty, dredles, deruely þer stondeȝ
Armed, ful aȝleȝ; in hert hit hym lykeȝ.
Þenn he meleȝ muryly wyth a much steuen,
And wyth a rynkande rurde he to þe renk sayde:
'Bolde burne, on þis bent be not so gryndel.
No mon here vnmanerly þe mysboden habbeȝ,
Ne kyd bot as couenaunde at kyngeȝ kort schaped.
I hyȝt þe a strok and þou hit hatȝ, halde þe wel payed;
I relece þe of þe remnaunt of ryȝtes alle oþer.
Iif I deliuer had bene, a boffet paraunter
I couþe wroþeloker haf waret, to þe haf wroȝt anger.
Fyrst I mansed þe muryly with a mynt one,
And roue þe wyth no rof-sore, with ryȝt I þe profered
For þe forwarde þat we fest in þe fyrst nyȝt,
And þou trystyly þe trawþe and trwly me haldeȝ,
Al þe gayne þow me gef, as god mon schulde.
Þat oþer munt for þe morne, mon, I þe profered,
Þou kyssedes my clere wyf, þe cosseȝ me raȝteȝ.
For boþe two here I þe bede bot two bare myntes
boute scaþe.
Trwe mon trwe restore,
Þenne þar mon drede no waþe.
At þe þrid þou fayled þore,
And þerfor þat tappe ta þe.

'For hit is my wede þat þou wereȝ, þat ilke wouen girdel;
Myn owen wyf hit þe weued, I wot wel for soþe.
Now know I wel þy cosses and þy costes als,
And þe wowyng of my wyf; I wroȝt hit myseluen.
I sende hir to asay þe, and sothly me þynkkeȝ
On þe fautlest freke þat euer on fote ȝede;
As perle bi þe quite pese is of prys more,
So is Gawayn, in god fayth, bi oþer gay knyȝteȝ.
Bot here yow lakked a lyttel, sir, and lewté yow wonted;
Bot þat watȝ for no wylyde werke, ne wowyng nauþer,
Bot for ȝe lufed your lyf; þe lasse I yow blame.'
Þat oþer stif mon in study stod a gret whyle,

The man stood back from him and rested on his axe, setting the handle on the ground and leaning on the blade, and gazed at the knight standing there in the glade, noting how that brave man, undaunted, stood there boldly in his armour, quite without fear; at heart the sight pleased him. Then he spoke cheerfully in a loud voice, and with a ringing tone he said to the knight: 'Valiant knight, you need not be so fierce on this battlefield. No one has improperly abused you here, nor acted otherwise than as the covenant made at the king's court laid down. I promised you one blow and you have had it, so consider yourself paid in full; I release you from all remaining obligations whatsoever. If I had been ready to I could perhaps have dealt you a blow more harshly, and have done you harm. First I threatened you playfully with a single feinted blow, without inflicting a serious wound, treating you fairly in accordance with the agreement which we made on the first evening, and you, loyally and honestly keeping faith with me, gave me all your winnings, as a true man should. The second feint, sir, I offered you for the following day, when you kissed my lovely wife, and gave me the kisses. For both those days I just now offered you merely two feints without harm done. An honest man must make honest reparation, then need he fear no danger. On the third day you failed in that respect, and for that you must suffer that trifling wound.

'For it is my garment you are wearing, that woven girdle there; I know for certain my own wife gave it to you. Moreover, I know all about your kisses and your conduct too, and my wife's wooing of you; I myself brought it about. I sent her to put you to the proof, and truly you seem to me the most faultless knight who ever lived; as a pearl in comparison with a dried pea is of greater value, so, truthfully, is Gawain beside other gallant knights. Yet in this you were a little at fault sir, and lacking in fidelity; but that was not for any excellence of workmanship in the girdle, nor because of wooing either, but because you loved your life; I blame you the less for that.' The other bold man stood a long while in silent thought, so overcome with mortification

So agreued for greme he gryed withinne;
Alle þe blode of his brest blende in his face,
Þat al he schrank for schome þat þe schalk talked.
Þe forme worde vpon folde þat þe freke meled:
'Corsed worth cowarddyse and couetyse boþe!
In yow is vylany and vyse þat vertue disstryeȝ.'
Þenne he kaȝt to þe knot and þe kest lawseȝ,
Brayde broþely þe belt to þe burne seluen:
'Lo! þer þe falssyng, foule mot hit falle!
For care of þy knokke cowardyse me taȝt
To acorde me with couetyse, my kynde to forsake,
Þat is larges and lewté þat longeȝ to knyȝteȝ.
Now am I fawty and falce, and ferde haf ben euer
Of trecherye and vntrawþe—boþe bityde sorȝe
and care!
I biknowe yow, knyȝt, here stylle,
Al fawty is my fare;
Leteȝ me ouertake your wylle,
And efte I schal be ware.'

Thenn loȝe þat oþer leude and lufyly sayde:
'I halde hit hardily hole, þe harme þat I hade.
Þou art confessed so clene, beknowen of þy mysses,
And hatȝ þe penaunce apert of þe poynt of myn egge,
I halde þe polysed of þat plyȝt and pured as clene
As þou hadeȝ neuer forfeted syþen þou watȝ fyrst borne.
And I gif þe, sir, þe gurdel þat is golde-hemmed;
For hit is grene as my goune, Sir Gawayn, ȝe maye
Þenk vpon þis ilke þrepe þer þou forth þryngeȝ
Among prynces of prys, and þis a pure token
Of þe chaunce of þe grene chapel at cheualrous knyȝteȝ.
And ȝe schal in þis Nwe Ȝer aȝayn to my woneȝ,
And we schyn reuel þe remnaunt of þis ryche fest
ful bene.'
Þer laþed hym fast þe lorde
And sayde: 'With my wyf, I wene,
We schal yow wel acorde,
Þat watȝ your enmy kene.'

that he shuddered inwardly; all his heart's blood rushed into his face, so that his whole being winced with shame at what the man had said. The first words the knight actually spoke were: 'A curse upon cowardice and avarice too! In you is ill-breeding and vice which destroy knightly virtue.' Then he laid hold of the knot and, loosening the fastening, angrily flung the belt straight at the man: 'See, there is the token of my broken faith, bad luck to it! Because I feared your blow, cowardice led me to have to do with covetousness, to forsake my true nature, that generosity and fidelity which is proper to knights. Now I am lacking in fidelity and guilty of breach of faith, I who have always abhorred treachery and dishonesty—may sorrow and care befall both of them! I here humbly confess to you, sir, that my behaviour is very sinful; let me understand your pleasure with respect to penance, and henceforth I will be on my guard.'

Then the other laughed and said amiably: 'I count it wholly atoned for, such injury as I received. You are made so clean by confession, by admission of your faults, and having openly done penance at the point of my blade, I consider you absolved of that offence and purged as clean as if you had never sinned since the day you were born. And I will give you, sir, the girdle edged with gold; because it is green like my tunic, Sir Gawain, you may remember this contest of ours when you have made your way back among noble princes, and this will be a perfect token, in the company of chivalrous knights, of the adventure of the Green Chapel. And you must come back again to my dwelling at this New Year season, and we shall revel very pleasantly for the remainder of this high festival.' The lord pressingly invited him there, saying: 'We will, I know, reconcile you perfectly with my wife, who was your keen opponent.'

'Nay, for soþe,' quoþ þe segge, and sesed hys helme
And hatȝ hit of hendely and þe haþel þonkkeȝ,
'I haf soiorned sadly; sele yow bytyde,
And he ȝelde hit yow ȝare þat ȝarkkeȝ al menskes!
And comaundeȝ me to þat cortays, your comlych fere,
Boþe þat on and þat oþer, myn honoured ladyeȝ,
Þat þus hor knyȝt wyth hor kest han koyntly bigyled.
Bot hit is no ferly þaȝ a fole madde
And þurȝ wyles of wymmen be wonen to sorȝe,
For so watȝ Adam in erde with one bygyled,
And Salamon with fele sere, and Samson eftsoneȝ—
Dalyda dalt hym hys wyrde—and Dauyth þerafter
Watȝ blended with Barsabe, þat much bale þoled.
Now þese were wrathed wyth her wyles, hit were a wynne huge
To luf hom wel and leue hem not, a leude þat couþe.
For þes wer forne þe freest, þat folȝed alle þe sele
Excellently of alle þyse oþer, vnder heuenryche
þat mused;
And alle þay were biwyled
With wymmen þat þay vsed.
Þaȝ I be now bigyled,
Me þink me burde be excused.

'Bot your gordel,' quoþ Gawayn, 'God yow forȝelde!
Þat wyl I welde wyth guod wylle, not for þe wynne golde,
Ne þe saynt, ne þe sylk, ne þe syde pendaundes,
For wele ne for worchyp, ne for þe wlonk werkkeȝ,
Bot in syngne of my surfet I schal se hit ofte,
When I ride in renoun, remorde to myseluen
Þe faut and þe fayntyse of þe flesche crabbed,
How tender hit is to entyse teches of fylþe;
And þus, quen pryde schal me pryk for prowes of armes,
Þe loke to þis luf-lace schal leþe my hert.
Bot on I wolde yow pray, displeses yow neuer:
Syn ȝe be lorde of þe ȝonder londe þer I haf lent inne
Wyth yow wyth worschyp—þe wyȝe hit yow ȝelde
Þat vphaldeȝ þe heuen and on hyȝ sitteȝ—
How norne ȝe yowre ryȝt nome, and þenne no more?'
'Þat schal I telle þe trwly,' quoþ þat oþer þenne;
'Bertilak de Hautdesert I hat in þis londe.

'No, indeed,' said the knight, and, seizing his helmet and courteously removing it, he thanked the lord, 'I have stayed long enough; good fortune befall you, and may He who bestows all honours reward you fully! And commend me to that gracious lady, your lovely wife, both to her and to the other also, those ladies whom I honour, who have so cleverly deceived their knight with their trickery. But it is no wonder if a fool behaves foolishly and is brought to grief through the wiles of women, for Adam while on earth was thus beguiled by one, and Solomon by many different women, and also Samson—Delilah dealt him his doom—and David was similarly deluded by Bathsheba and suffered great misery. Now since these were brought to grief by the wiles of women, it would be far better to love them well and trust them never, if one only could. For these were the noblest men of old, those who were pre-eminently favoured by fortune, above all others who lived beneath the heavens; and all these were deceived by women with whom they had relations. If now I am deluded, it seems to me I ought to be excused.

'As for your girdle,' said Gawain, 'God give you thanks for it! That will I keep willingly, not for the sake of its fair gold, nor for the belt itself, the silk, or the dangling pendants, nor for its costliness, for its worth, nor for its splendid workmanship, but in token of my transgression I shall often look at it, when I ride in honour, to remind myself with remorse of the sinfulness and the frailty of the erring flesh, how liable it is to catch the plague spots of sin; and so, when pride of my prowess in arms shall stir in me, one glance at this love-lace will humble my heart. But one thing I would beg of you, do not be offended at it: since you are the lord of that land in which I stayed with you and was honourably entertained—may the One who upholds the heavens and is throned on high reward you for it—how are you called by your proper name? and then I will ask you nothing more.' 'That I will tell you truly,' said the other in reply; 'in this country I am called Bertilak de Hautdesert.

Þurȝ myȝt of Morgne la Faye, þat in my hous lenges,
And koyntyse of clergye bi craftes wel lerned,
Þe maystrés of Merlyn mony hatȝ taken—
For ho hatȝ dalt drwry ful dere sumtyme
With þat conable klerk, þat knowes alle your knyȝteȝ
at hame;
Morgne þe goddes
Þerfore hit is hir name:
Weldeȝ non so hyȝe hawtesse
Þat ho ne con make ful tame—

'Ho wayned me vpon þis wyse to your wynne halle
For to assay þe surquidré, ȝif hit soth were
Þat rennes of þe grete renoun of þe Rounde Table.
Ho wayned me þis wonder your wytteȝ to reue,
For to haf greued Gaynour and gart hir to dyȝe
With glopnyng of þat ilke gome þat gostlych speked
With his hede in his honde bifore þe hyȝe table.
Þat is ho þat is at home, þe auncian lady;
Ho is euen þyn aunt, Arþureȝ half-suster,
Þe duches doȝter of Tyntagelle, þat dere Vter after
Hade Arþur vpon, þat aþel is nowþe.
Þerfore I eþe þe, haþel, to com to þyn aunt,
Make myry in my hous; my meny þe louies,
And I wol þe as wel, wyȝe, bi my faythe,
As any gome vnder God, for þy grete trauþe.'
And he nikked hym naye, he nolde bi no wayes.
Þay acolen and kyssen, and kennen ayþer oþer
To þe prynce of paradise, and parten ryȝt þere
on coolde;
Gawayn on blonk ful bene
To þe kyngeȝ burȝ buskeȝ bolde,
And þe knyȝt in þe enker-grene
Whiderwarde-so-euer he wolde.

2448 hatȝ: MS ho
2461 glopnyng: MS gopnyng gome: MS gomen
2472 and kennen *supplied*

Through the power of Morgan le Fay, who dwells in my house, and by her wiles has learned much skill in magic lore, has acquired many of the miraculous powers of Merlin—for she once had very intimate love-dealings with that accomplished wizard, as all your knights at home will know; and so Morgan the goddess is her name; there is no one so arrogantly proud whom she cannot humble utterly —

'it was she who sent me to your splendid hall in this guise to put your presumption to the test, to see whether what is rumoured about the great renown of the Round Table were true. She sent this marvel to rob you all of your wits, in order to shock Guinevere and cause her to die of terror at that man who, like a phantom, stood talking before the high table with his head in his hand. That venerable lady in my home is she; she is actually your aunt, Arthur's half-sister, daughter of the Duchess of Tintagel, upon whom the noble Uther later begot Arthur, who is now king. And so I entreat you, sir, to come to your aunt, and make merry in my house; my household all love you, and I, sir, bear you as much good will, upon my honour, as I do any man on earth, because of your great integrity.' But Gawain refused him, saying he would not on any account. Embracing and kissing, they commended each other to the Prince of Paradise and parted right there amidst the snow; Gawain on his fine steed quickly hastening to the king's castle, and the knight in green going wheresoever he wished.

Wylde wayeȝ in þe worlde Wowen now rydeȝ
On Gryngolet, þat þe grace hade geten of his lyue.
Ofte he herbered in house and ofte al þeroute,
And mony aventure in vale, and venquyst ofte,
Þat I ne tyȝt at þis tyme in tale to remene.
Þe hurt watȝ hole þat he hade hent in his nek,
And þe blykkande belt he bere þeraboute,
Abelef as a bauderyk, bounden bi his syde,
Loken vnder his lyfte arme, þe lace, with a knot,
In tokenyng he watȝ tane in tech of a faute.
And þus he commes to þe court, knyȝt al in sounde.
Þer wakned wele in þat wone when wyst þe grete
Þat gode Gawayn watȝ commen; gayn hit hym þoȝt.
Þe kyng kysseȝ þe knyȝt, and þe whene alce,
And syþen mony syker knyȝt þat soȝt hym to haylce,
Of his fare þat hym frayned; and ferlyly he telles,
Biknoweȝ alle þe costes of care þat he hade,
Þe chaunce of þe chapel, þe chere of þe knyȝt,
Þe luf of þe ladi, þe lace at þe last.
Þe nirt in þe nek he naked hem schewed,
Þat he laȝt for his vnleuté at þe leudes hondes
for blame.
He tened quen he schulde telle,
He groned for gref and grame;
Þe blod in his face con melle,
When he hit schulde schewe, for schame.

'Lo! lorde,' quoþ þe leude, and þe lace hondeled,
'Þis is þe bende of þis blame I bere in my nek,
Þis is þe laþe and þe losse þat I laȝt haue
Of couardise and couetyse þat I haf caȝt þare.
Þis is þe token of vntrawþe þat I am tan inne,
And I mot nedeȝ hit were wyle I may last;
For mon may hyden his harme, bot vnhap ne may hit,
For þer hit oneȝ is tachched twynne wil hit neuer.'
Þe kyng comforteȝ þe knyȝt, and alle þe court als
Laȝen loude þerat, and luflyly acorden
Þat lordes and ledes þat longed to þe Table,

2506 in *supplied* 2511 mon: MS non
2515 ledes: MS ladis

Now Gawain, whose life had graciously been spared, went riding upon Gryngolet by wild pathways through the world. Often he sheltered in a house and often found no shelter whatsoever, having many adventures by the way, and many victories, which at this point in the tale I do not intend to recount. The wound which he had received in his neck was healed, and he wore the shining belt over it, slung diagonally like a baldric, fastened at his side, the girdle being tied under his left arm with a knot, in order to signify that he had been detected in a guilty fault. And so the knight came safe and sound to court. There was joy in that dwelling when the nobles learnt that the good Sir Gawain had returned; it seemed wonderful to them. The king kissed the knight, and the queen also, and then many trusty knights who had come to greet him and ask him how he had fared; and he told his amazing story, confessed all the tribulations which he had suffered, the strange occurrence at the chapel, the behaviour of the Green Knight, the lady's wooing, and finally about the belt. He uncovered and showed them the scratch on his neck, which he had received at the knight's hands as a rebuke for his lack of fidelity. He suffered torment when he had to speak of it, he groaned with grief and mortification; the blood rushed into his face for shame, when he had to confess it.

'See! my lord,' said the knight, touching the girdle, 'this is the blazon of this guilty scar I bear in my neck, this is the badge of the injury and the harm which I have received because of the cowardice and covetousness to which I there fell prey. This is the token of the perfidy in which I have been detected, and I must needs wear it as long as I may live; for one may conceal one's offence, but cannot undo it, for once it has become fixed it will never leave one.' The king consoled the knight, and all the court likewise laughed loudly over it, and agreed for friendship's sake that the lords and knights who belonged to the

Vche burne of þe broþerhede, a bauderyk schulde haue,
A bende abelef hym aboute of a bryȝt grene,
And þat, for sake of þat segge, in swete to were.
For þat watȝ acorded þe renoun of þe Rounde Table,
And he honoured þat hit hade, euermore after,
As hit is breued in þe best boke of romaunce.
Þus in Arthurus day þis aunter bitidde,
Þe Brutus bokeȝ þerof beres wyttenesse.
Syþen Brutus, þe bolde burne, boȝed hider fyrst,
After þe segge and þe asaute watȝ sesed at Troye,
iwysse,
Mony aunttereȝ here-biforne
Haf fallen suche er þis.
Now þat bere þe croun of þorne,
He bryng vus to his blysse! AMEN

HONY SOYT QUI MAL PENCE

Round Table, every member of the brotherhood, should have a baldric, a band of bright green worn crosswise about him, and, for the knight's sake, to wear it just like him. For the good repute of the Round Table was associated with it, and ever afterwards anyone who wore it was honoured, as is written in the best books of romance. Thus in the days of Arthur befell this adventure, of which the chronicles of Britain bear record. Since Brutus, that valiant man, first came here, after the siege and the assault had ended at Troy, truly, many such adventures have occurred in times past. And now may He who wore the crown of thorns bring us to His bliss! AMEN

HONI SOIT QUI MAL Y PENSE

discordance between reaction of K of the RT, + triumphant tone of last few lines, + Gawain's shame. No closure, not explanation.

Abbreviations

EDD	*The English Dialect Dictionary*, ed. Joseph Wright (London, 1898–1905).
OED	*The Oxford English Dictionary*, ed. Sir J. A. H. Murray, H. Bradley, Sir W. Craigie, C. T. Onions (Oxford, 1933).
MED	*Middle English Dictionary*, ed. H. Kurath, S. M. Kuhn, J. Reidy (Ann Arbor, Mich., 1952–).
TG	*Sir Gawain and the Green Knight*, ed. J. R. R. Tolkien and E. V. Gordon (Oxford, 1925; corrected reprint, 1946).
TGD	Second edition, revised by Norman Davis, 1967.
Goll.	*Sir Gawain and the Green Knight*, ed. Sir Israel Gollancz (London, EETS, OS 210, 1940).
Bur.	*Sir Gawain and the Green Knight*, ed. J. A. Burrow (Harmondsworth, Penguin Books, 1972).
Sil.	*Sir Gawain and the Green Knight*, ed. Theodore Silverstein (Chicago and London, 1984).
Wal.	*The Poems of the 'Pearl' Manuscript*, ed. Malcolm Andrew and Ronald Waldron (Exeter, 1987).
Van.	*Sir Gawain and the Green Knight: A Dual-Language Version*, ed. William Vantuono (New York and London, 1991).
And.	*Sir Gawain and the Green Knight, Pearl, Cleanness, Patience*, ed. J. J. Anderson (London, Everyman's Library, 1996).

Notes

1–19 The opening stanza contains a characteristic combination of the verbal and thematic ambiguities which make the poem so fascinating to read, so difficult to translate. Its overt subject is the foundation of European civilisations by noble refugees from fallen Troy, of medieval chivalry by the heroes of antiquity. The *tulk* of line 3 must surely be Aeneas, the archetypal founding father, but his *tresoun* is ambiguous. According to the medieval versions of the Troy legend, Aeneas helped Antenor to betray the city to the Greeks but, out of compassion, concealed from them the princess Polyxena, whom they wished to sacrifice on Achilles' tomb; Antenor revealed her hiding place, and the Greeks, incensed at Aeneas' bad faith, sent him into exile. To medieval readers, who were pro-Trojan in their sympathies, Aeneas' deception of the Greeks was admirable, yet his treachery to Troy was manifest—indeed, it may well be his *tricherie* rather than himself which is described as *þe trewest on erthe*, 'the most patent known to man' (*cf.* And.). And, the context implies, the same ambiguity of reputation has been inherited by Britain, founded *with wynne* (joy) by his legendary great-grandson *Felix* (fortunate) Brutus, yet torn by *werre and wrake and wonder*, forever alternating between *blysse and blunder*.

The relevance of this introduction to a story in which the reputation of the Round Table and its noblest representative, Gawain, is to be tested and found admirable yet imperfect is obvious. Whether the reader's attention is to be directed to reputation or to the testing of a hero depends upon the interpretation of *tried* (l. 4). Some editors gloss it as p.p. 'tried (for crime)', others as adj. 'of proven quality, distinguished, famous'. Both senses are present in the root meaning of the verb, 'to distinguish (one thing) from another by testing'; and both are, perhaps, invoked here to suggest that success may be relative and reputation ambiguous, that *tresoun* may make a man famous in some eyes, notorious in others. Which Aeneas should be regarded as is irrelevant; indeed, the *tulk* is never explicitly identified—*Hit watȝ* … could either have no reference to the first four lines or, alternatively, be interpreted 'Yet it was this Aeneas who …' It is rather the general implications which are important: the irony implicit in the ambiguous association of *tresoun*, *tried* and *trewest* is extended throughout this introductory passage by the language applied to Aeneas and the other founders of European nations (*athel*, *highe kynde*, *depreced*, *riche*, *bobbaunce*, *Felix*). The reader is, perhaps, being alerted to ironic overtones in what follows, a story of Western chivalry and its values.

22 **turned** (p.p. as adj.) has various senses corresponding to those of the verb, amongst which OED gives (under 111) 'to change or reverse position', and hence (adj., 6(b)) 'reversed so as to be upside down'. In reference to an age when 'bold warriors ..., lovers of strife, ... made mischief', this suggests 'topsy-turvy, unsettled, troubled'. *Cf.* And.

33–6 Opinions differ as to whether or not there is an allusion here to the alliterative medium in which the poem is written or merely to the pre-existence of its story-matter. *Loken* ('linked, fastened'), paralleling *stoken*, obviously refers to the story, not the medium; *letteres* can be either the alphabetic characters or the writings they compose; *lel* ('correct, exact') could refer either to the fitness of the words to express the matter or to the matching of initial letters in the alliterative scheme. If the latter, one might translate: 'framed in letters fitly linked together, as has long been (the practice) in this land'.

The alliterative medium, remotely descended from the Anglo-Saxon verse form, survived the cultural shock of the Norman conquest—no one knows how—to serve, in a variety of forms, for a remarkable body of poetry composed in the north and west during the fourteenth century. Its basic characteristic is a long line divided by a caesura (||), each half containing two strongly stressed syllables (′) and a variable number of unstressed syllables (×), the whole linked together by repetition of the initial sounds of two or more of the stressed syllables (alliteration):

′ × × × ′ × || × ′ × × ′ ×
Ticius to **T**uskan and **t**eldes bigynnes

The link may sometimes consist of vowels alliterating with each other or with initial *h*, and occasionally there is a double alliterative pattern:

And wyth a **c**ountenaunce **d**ryȝe he **d**roȝ doun his **c**ote

In *Gawain*, uniquely, the long lines are grouped in stanzas of varying length, each rounded off by a one-stress line followed by a quatrain of three-stress lines showing alliteration and rhyming together *ababa*. The free flow of the long lines, the relation of their changing stress patterns to those of natural speech, the varying emphasis of alliteration, sometimes casual, sometimes insistent, make this an ideal medium for oral story-telling. The verse paragraphs avoid monotony, the quatrain sometimes summarising epigrammatically, sometimes delivering a shock or implying an enigma to draw the reader onward.

43 **caroles to make** The specific sense of *carole* is 'a round-dance accompanied by singing', but OED (*carol* n., 1(b)) lists this occurrence under the more general sense 'diversions or merry-making, of which such dances formed a leading feature', citing also *The Ayenbyte of Inwyt* 71: 'Oure blisse is ywent into wop, owre karoles into zorȝe'. Editors have generally preferred the specific sense, but in association with the verb *make* and in a context where various diversions, including dancing, are indicated, the more general meaning seems preferable.

61 **on þe dece** In the common hall of medieval castles, as in some college dining halls today, the principal table, running across the top of the room, was placed on a raised platform or dais. Those of noblest rank sat at this 'high' table, and the adjective referred rather to the honour of such a position than to its elevation. Here, as elsewhere, *dece is* used as a synonym for 'high table', but probably refers also to the tables filling the body of the hall at which the lesser nobles were served, since any discrimination in service at a New Year feast seems unlikely. After all the 'high table' company had dined, the lower tables would be filled by lesser persons at second and third sittings. The poet perhaps preferred this arrangement of tables because it would help contemporary readers to visualise the scene, or because the Round Table of Arthurian tradition would prevent the Green Knight from riding into the middle of the company to issue his challenge.

66–70 It has usually been assumed that this passage involves both the giving of gifts (perhaps by the nobles to the servants) and the playing of a game (perhaps handy-dandy) in which some win and others lose. The assumption rests upon an apparent distinction between *giftes* and *hondeselle* ('largesse given to inferiors'). But though the root sense of the latter may have been 'that which is given into the hands of another' it had more specific meanings in the later Middle Ages: '(*a*) a token or indication of luck, good or bad; fortune, luck; (*b*) something given (especially in the New Year) as a token of good luck; also *fig.*; (*c*) payment, reward' (MED *hanselle* n.). It seems possible that in this context the primitive sense is combined with something of both (*a*) and (*b*): a New Year token, of good luck or ill, proffered in the hand so that another can guess its identity or which hand contains it. If the tokens were conceived of as small gifts offered by the men and given to the ladies who guessed correctly, while those who guessed wrongly paid the forfeit of a kiss, the passage as a whole would make sense. The ambiguity is probably deliberate, since a game with forfeits and involving a sexual element is at the heart of the poem, yet its meaning must not be apparent until much later.

151–60 The Green Knight, having come on a peaceful mission *(cf.* 271), wears the normal dress of a gentleman at leisure: a short, close-fitting tunic under a hooded cape lined with fur, and skin-tight hose worn with spurs but without shoes, as manuscript illustrations show us they sometimes were for riding or hunting.

199 **loked** here seems to be used in the sense identified by OED (*look* v., 1(c)) as 'to direct one's eyes in a manner indicative of a certain feeling; to cast a look of a certain significance; to present a specified expression of countenance'. *Cf.* MED *loken* v.[2] and Wal. *Layt* is usually glossed 'lightning', more rarely 'flash of fire' (OED *lait* n.; *cf.* MED *leit* n.[1](b)); the latter seems more appropriate to a glance.

206–8 A branch carried in the hand was a sign of peace (*cf.* 265-6). The contrast between the evergreen holly, symbol of Christmas hope, and the monstrous axe in his other hand typifies the ambiguous presentation of the Green Knight: handsome yet abnormal in stature, elegantly dressed yet peculiar in colouring, without armour yet of menacing appearance.

237–45 Those standing around are presumably servants. Their rapid, if superficial, identification of the Green Knight's appearance as 'illusion and enchantment' contrasts with the stunned silence of the nobles, increasing the reader's uncertainty as to how the strange figure is to be interpreted.

246–9 The poet's comment on politeness as a possible explanation for the courtiers' silence is more obviously ironic if *let* is taken not as 'allowed' but in the sense 'to leave *to* someone else' (OED v.[1], 4).

250 **auenture** is normally applied to events, especially any accidental, dangerous or mysterious occurrence; hence 'a prodigy, a marvel' (OED *adventure* n., 5). Here 'apparition' seems a suitable variant, since the reference is to a person, though one whose nature, human or supernatural, has not yet been made clear.

265–84 The translation of two terms here depends upon the overall interpretation of the passage. *In fere* (267) normally means 'in company' and, in military contexts, 'with a company of fighting men'. But the Green Knight is unaccompanied, and in *Rauf Coilȝear* 702 the expression is used of a knight fighting alone; perhaps, having been long applied to the company of fighting men, it had come to mean generally 'in martial fashion' *(cf.* TGD, And., Wal.). To accept such a meaning here would make the following phrase, *in feȝtyng wyse*, tautological. The Green Knight is surely stating a hypothesis, not a fact: had he sought a fight he would have come with a company and in arms. Is Arthur responding to the first qualification or the second when he offers *batayl bare* (277)? The adjective frequently implies 'unarmed' (MED *bar* adj., 2(a)), but if Arthur offers unarmed combat there seems no point in the Green Knight's statement (279–82) that no member of the Round Table could match him in arms. One of the root meanings of the word is 'without anything in the nature of addition' (OED 111) and the context here suggests 'single combat' (MED 13(d); *cf.* Van. trans.), supported by the use of the adjective in *þre bare mote* (1141), 'three single notes'.

296 **barlay** is an obscure term usually identified with the modern dialect *barley*, used by children to call a temporary truce in games or to lay first claim to something ('bags I'). The interjection is presumably related to the verb meaning 'to claim by right of first choice' (EDD *barley* v.). As the Green Knight has already stated that he will receive the first blow (290, 294), it seems less likely that he is claiming that (Goll., Wal.) than establishing his right to claim the return blow (And., TGD).

347 **to your counseyl** 'To advise you' (TGD gloss.; *cf.* And. gloss., Wal.) is not in keeping with Gawain's punctilious deference to the king. His suggestion appears more discreet if the noun is taken as 'the act of discussing or conferring' (MED *counseil* n., 2).

360 If **rych** is taken as an adjective following its noun (as at 20, 243, etc.), the sense is 'Even if *I* speak improperly let all this noble court be free from blame' (TGD). But why should Arthur blame the court for any impropriety on Gawain's part? If *rych* is the rare verb used at 1223 (Goll. gloss. 'direct'; OED *rich* v.^{2}, 4 'advise'; 6 'adjust, settle'), here it may mean 'decide' (Goll. gloss., Wal.), and if *bout blame* is taken in the sense 'without giving offence' (MED *blame* n., 1(a)), there is reasonable preparation for the court's decision which immediately follows (362–5).

409 **frayst my fare** has been translated 'try my behaviour', 'see what I will do' (TGD) and 'call on me' (Wal.), but if the verb is taken as 'to enquire' (MED *fraisten* v., 4(a)) and *fare* as 'condition, state of affairs' (MED n.^{1}, 7(a)), a translation is possible—'enquire after my welfare'— which allows the Green Knight to echo ironically the thought in Arthur's mind (372–4) and possibly in Gawain's (383–5): that he will be in no fit condition to strike the return blow. Cf. Goll.

471–3 As the emphasis here is on the suitability of interludes—short dramatic entertainments originally given between the courses of a banquet—and other pastimes to the Christmas season, *kynde* may be taken as 'required by nature, appropriate, suitable, proper' (MED adj., 1(d)), i.e. proper to the season.

476–7 Arthur uses the proverbial expression 'Heng vp þyn ax' both literally and figuratively—'Have done with this affair'. *Gaynly*, 'suitably, fittingly' (MED *geinli* adv., 2(b)), draws attention to the word-play.

489 **frayn** has generally been translated 'seek out' (Goll. gloss.) or 'make trial of' (TGD gloss., Wal.), but the sense recorded by MED (*frainen* v., 5) as 'to seek (adventure, battle), to quest' seems more appropriate (And.).

491–9 The opening of the second section of the poem, which exploits and extends some of the ambiguities implicit in the first, may be read at several levels. A more explicit reading might begin: 'This omen of strange events to come Arthur received at the beginning, when the year was young, because he had longed to receive a challenge.' The use here of *hanselle* (see note on 66–70), reminding us of its earlier association with New Year gifts and with a game whose implications are dubious, the supernatural overtones of *auenturus* (see note on 250), the ambiguity of *ȝelpyng* ('boasting, proud or pompous talk' (OED *yelping* 1)), alluding both to the court's vaunting pride in chivalric exploit and to the Green Knight's answering challenge (see 309–12), and the grim emphasis of *stafful* ('as full as one's hand is in holding a staff' (OED *staff-full*), perhaps an ironic allusion to the Green Knight's axe in Gawain's hands), all suggest the possibility of darker implications in what follows: the antithesis of 'happy' and 'sad', 'beginning' and 'end', the hint that the 'game' which has already proved to be no game was begun under the influence of drink, and the inexorable turning of the year whose end may be very different from its beginning.

520 **bide** is usually glossed 'to wait for', but 'to enjoy (food, love, luck)' (MED *biden* v., 8(c)) seems more appropriate to the rapid onward development of the action here. *Cf.* TGD.

533 **wage** 'forewarning'. The implications for the future, inherent in the noun ('a pledge of security' (OED n., 1)), are brought out in the verb: 'to give pledges or pledge oneself for the fulfilment of (something promised)' (OED v., 3).

547 **neuer bot trifel** is usually taken as Gawain's offhand way of dismissing the difficulties of his mission: 'it is only a minor matter' (Wal.); 'except for a small point'—his imminent departure (TGD). There are, however, indications (534–5, 562–5, 668–9) that his stiff upper lip conceals concern for the outcome; but since the mission cannot, with honour, be avoided, it is presumably *talking* about it that Gawain finds a *trifel*: 'a false or idle tale; a foolish, trivial or nonsensical saying' (OED *trifle* n., 1).

550–5 Those present at Gawain's departure, and therefore associated with the court's attitude to it, include some of the most eminent figures of the Arthurian world. The lesser-known Sir Dodinel is properly *le Sauvage*, so named for his love of hunting in wild forests, while Mador *de la Port is* apparently thought of as the royal gate-keeper.

558 **derne** ('secret') may be read as *derue* ('bitter') and *driuen* may be glossed 'experienced, felt' (MED *driven* v., 10(a)) or 'made, expressed' (MED 9). But the members of the court seem anxious to conceal their concern for Gawain from the knight (see 539–42), and only express their feelings openly to each other after his departure (672–81).

587 **pryde** 'pomp, ostentation, display' (OED *pride* n., 6).

608–14 The details of the embroidery on the silken band which attaches the chain-mail neck-guard to Gawain's helmet are of more than decorative importance. The parrots, the turtle-doves, the true-love flowers were all associated in the medieval arts with love. That the ladies of the court should choose to embroider them on Gawain's *vrysoun* would have surprised no reader of romance: his reputation as a perfect knight rested partly on his skill in the social arts of chivalry, refined conversation, dalliance and courtship, and he was first renowned, later notorious, for his amorous conquests. This oblique reminder of the amorous Gawain, in a context which stresses his physical and spiritual ideals by a detailed description of armour and heraldic bearing, is in preparation for his reception by the inhabitants of Bertilak's castle as the 'perfect master of good breeding' (see 915–27) and by the lady there as one from whom she might expect to learn 'some lessons in the arts of true love' (1527).

619–65 The pentangle, used as a symbol of health by the Pythagoreans and of perfection by the Neoplatonists and Gnostics, was often identified during the Middle Ages with 'Solomon's seal', traditionally a six-pointed star within a circle. Here it is the unity of the figure which is stressed, iconographically (628–30) and symbolically (656–61): *þe endeles knot* is a symbol of *trawþe*, a complex term best expressed, perhaps, by 'integrity'. The poet's attempt to expound the complex

of qualities, physical, spiritual and social, which constitute his hero's integrity by relating them to the fivefold structure of the pentangle (640–55) is somewhat strained and perhaps not yet fully understood. The effect is weakened by translation, which cannot reproduce some of the original word-plays: *poyntes* (627, 658), referring both to the 'angles' of the figure (MED *pointe* n.[1] 12(c)) and to the associated 'good qualities, virtues' (*ibid.*, 10(c)); *croked* (653), implying 'crooked, out of true' in relation to the lines of the pentangle, as well as 'morally deficient'; and *fetled* (656), meaning 'shaped' in the figure as well as 'bestowed' upon the man. The chivalric virtues of 651–5 are complex qualities and each is very inadequately expressed by any single term in modern English.

673 **soþly** Normally 'with truth', but here, perhaps, 'softly, quietly', since open criticism of the king by his courtiers seems unlikely. *Cf.* 'a sooth whisper' (EDD *sooth* adj.[2]), and *Purity* (ed. Menner) 654, 'And sayde sothly to hirself', where it translates Latin *occulte*; so also Bur.

691–702 Gawain's journey takes him from Camelot, somewhere in the south, through the Arthurian kingdom of Logres, into north Wales, where the geography of romance becomes that of reality as he approaches the region in which the poet and his original audience lived. Following a known medieval route, Gawain keeps Anglesey and the neighbouring small islands on his left, and rides east along the coast of north Wales, crossing various rivers where they enter the sea, then the estuary of the Dee at a point not certainly identified, then the Wirral, notorious for its outlaws in the fourteenth century. There he re-enters *contrayez straunge* (713), where the creatures of romance swarm (715–25) in the landscape and climate of the north (726–47).

773–6 Gawain appropriately thanks St Julian, patron saint of travellers, just as later (1788–91), in denying that he has a sweetheart, he swears by St John the Apostle, by tradition dedicated to celibacy. Similarly, the porter invokes St Peter (807–14), keeper of heaven's gate, and Bertilak the hunter swears by St Giles (1644), who befriended a hind.

800–2 The elaborate roofline of the castle, crowded with turrets, pinnacles and chimneys, may have reminded the poet of the table decorations and dish covers at medieval banquets: 'bake-metes and dissh-metes ... peynted and castelled with papir' (*Canterbury Tales*, x (1), 440–5); see also *Purity* 1405–8.

862–8 Gawain wears a long-skirted robe, perhaps slit at the sides, displaying his tight hose and the close sleeves of an under-tunic in contrasting colours.

1020–8 On the last day of the festival, apparently St John's Day, 27 December, the guests take leave at the end of the evening in order to depart early next morning (1126–32), before the lord goes hunting. The hunts occupy the last three days of the year (1965–8), so 28 December is unaccounted for. A line referring to it may have been lost between 1022 and 1023. On *caroles* see note on 43 above.

1150–77 The hunting of the deer, like that of the boar and the fox later, is exact and technical in description. Beaters accompanied by greyhounds drive the hinds down into the valley bottom, while the male deer, for whom winter is the close season, are allowed to escape. Huntsmen, concealed in the wood, shoot the driven deer with bow and arrow, while those who escape are pulled down by heavy greyhounds and their handlers on the edges of the area. The lord repeatedly rides ahead of the drive to dismount and shoot again.

1182–3 **sleȝly** is usually construed with *dyn*, 'heard a little stealthy sound', though the syntax is strained. A more natural relationship to *herde* may be possible if the adverb is understood in a derived sense, 'quietly, faintly, half-consciously' (*cf.* MED *sleighli* adv. (d), 'imperceptibly'). Alternatively, *sleȝly* may be a scribal error, perhaps for *sleȝtly*, 'without much care or attention, carelessly, lightly' (OED *slightly* adv., 2). This sense is not recorded before the sixteenth century, but the adjective 'slender, thin' is known from the fourteenth.

1237–40 The literal bluntness of the lady's offer, 'You are welcome to my body, to do (with it) as you please', can be avoided by taking *my cors* as a periphrasis for 'me', and the whole as a polite social formula whose tone is continued by the use of a technical term (*seruaunt*, 'devoted slave') from the language of courtly love. It is in this formal, social sense that Gawain chooses to respond to her declaration.

1263–7 This passage appears obscure, partly no doubt as a reflection of Gawain's confusion in face of the lady's compliments, possibly also because of textual corruption. Some editors add prepositions after *fongen* (1265): TGD, adding *bi* and taking the verb as past participle parallel to *founden* (1264), translates 'and received much else from other people by their actions'; And., adding *for*, reads 'and others receive a great deal (of respect) from other people for their deeds'. But *fongen* does not normally take prepositions, and a direct relationship to *dedes* seems possible, in a figurative sense of the basic meaning 'take, receive' (MED v., 4(c) 'receive (light) by reflection', 6 'assume or take on (a certain form, colour)')—*cf.* TG 'take their line of action'. The last word of 1266 is evidently corrupt. TGD, reading *nysen*, emends to *nys euen*: 'but the honour they assign to me, since my desert is not equal to it, is to the honour of yourself'. But it is difficult to see why the honour paid to Gawain by other people should reflect directly upon the lady.

Wal., reading *nyseu* and assuming the omission of the *er* abbreviation, suggests *nys euer*. 'but the honour which they bestow is not at all my deserving'. This interpretation, together with the hiatus which most editors assume after 1266, and the apparently deliberate ambiguity of the repeated *oþer* in 1265, allows Gawain to suggest that his reputation has been inflated by the tendency of some people to ape the enthusiasms of others, without directly imputing such insincerity to the lady.

1283–7 A difficult passage, possibly corrupt in the opening line, which—in the manuscript—reads: 'Þaȝ *I* were burde bryȝtest þe *burde* in mynde hade'. Some editors take the first half as a reflection on the lady's part, but disagree as to whether it should continue through the first half of the next line (TG, Van.), or whether its complement is merely implied—'still he would resist' (TGD). In either case the sudden intrusion of her point of view and equally abrupt return to that of the narrator is improbable. The emendation accepted here, originally proposed by an early editor (R. Morris, 1864; *cf.* Goll., Wal., Bur.), avoids the unlikely repetition of *burde*, misreading of which could have led the scribe to alter *ho* to *I*. He may also have been misled by the unfamiliar use of *in mynde hade*, here 'remember (someone)' (MED *haven* v., 5a(b)). The sense of the following lines is improved if *lode,* usually translated 'way, journey', is taken as 'behaviour, manner, conduct' (MED n., 2(c)); *cf. liflode* (MED n. 3(a)) 'moral conduct, behaviour'.

1331 **schyre** Adjective as noun, 'white (flesh)', referring presumably to the contrast between the gullet and the dark meat of the neck.

1347 **noumbles** 'numbles', offal from the back and loins of the deer.

1355 **þe corbeles fee** A piece of gristle from the end of the breastbone, traditionally thrown into a tree for the crows or ravens.

1377 **tayles** Literally 'tails', which, being left on the carcasses, served as tallies of the numbers killed in the hunt.

1431 **knot** Primarily a 'knot' or 'knob', and therefore here, perhaps, a 'mound' or 'little hill' (MED *knotte* n., 9); but also 'a small bundle' (MED 8(a)) or 'clump', and so, here and at 1434, 'thicket', which avoids repetition of the sense of *clyffe* and *knarre* and fits with the boar's habit of lying amongst thorns and bushes (*cf.* TGD 1419).

1461 **bate** 'baiting; being attacked or harassed' (MED n.^{2}); *cf.* And., Sil.

1472 **forȝate** 'to omit or neglect through inadvertence' (OED *forget* v., 2).

1501 **comaundement** 'bidding' (TGD, Goll. gloss.), but also 'the power to rule or control' (MED *commaundement* n., 4); *ben at commaundement*, 'be at (someone's) disposal'.

1502 **lach** Literally 'seize' and therefore here, perhaps, 'embrace' (MED *lacchen* v.^{1}, 2(b)). But the word is also used in a variety of figurative senses, and here the parallelism with *leue* may suggest 'take up, begin'.

1513 **þe lettrure of armes** The 'learning' (OED n., 2) or science proper to the knightly profession. But *lettrure* is also 'a written book' (MED n., 2(a)) and, with an adjective, 'holy scripture' (MED 1(b)); the context here, in particular 1515, suggests written principles.

1527 **tokeneȝ** The word means primarily 'an authenticating sign or characteristic aspect', but also 'a word or material object employed to authenticate a person, message, or communication; a password' (OED *token* n., 7), so here, perhaps, 'vital instruction, teaching, lesson'. *Cf.* 1486, 'teaching' (TGD gloss.), 'lesson' (And.).

1529 **herken** 'listen (to)', but more appropriately here 'pay attention, take heed' (MED *herkenen* v., 1a(a)).

1662–3 **towrast** is probably past participle of a verb *towrest*, 'wrested away (from what is right)' (*cf.* OED *wrast* n.), hence 'awry'; *cf.* Sil. 'twisted awry'. Taking *turned* as preterite subjunctive in the sense 'to pervert, misapply' (OED *turn* v., 14), we can read 'might be misinterpreted'. *Cf.* Wal.

1675 **pryme** 'Prime' was the first division of the medieval day, 6.00–9.00 a.m., specifically a canonical hour of the divine office celebrated about dawn.

1838 **chosen** is usually translated 'set out for' (Goll.) or 'undertaken' (And., TGD gloss.), but Gawain's earnest attitude to his mission may justify a more specialised interpretation here: 'to dedicate or devote oneself to (Christianity, etc.)' (MED *chesen* v., 4b(a)).

1849 **knit** is usually interpreted literally, 'woven into' (And.), 'entwined' (TGD gloss.), 'bound up' (Goll. gloss.), 'woven' (Wal. gloss.), but an abstract sense seems more appropriate to the mysterious properties connected with the girdle: 'associated with' (MED *knitten* v., 5(b)).

2025–9 Despite the manuscript *wedeȝ* (as at 987), the reference is clearly to Gawain's surcoat (*cf.* Bur.), his noblest garment since it has his armorial bearing surrounded by *vertuus stoneȝ*—jewels were regarded as 'potent' (OED *virtuous* adj., 6) in the Middle Ages because of the magical or medicinal properties attributed to them. Their association with the hero's coat of arms adds to the irony of the juxtaposition of the pentangle and girdle (2030–6), since retention of the latter implies a breach of the virtues symbolised by the former; the badge, however potent its jewels, has not protected him from evil, and his faith now seems to have been transferred to the lace (2037–42). Gawain, however, appears quite unconscious of any impropriety.

2111 **may þe knyȝt rede** 'if the knight has his way'. The title seems inconsistent with the guide's picture of the violent and brutal guardian of the chapel. If, as has been suggested, the text originally read *may [y] þe, knyȝt, rede*, an acceptable translation is possible: 'I may warn you, knight'. *Cf.* TGD.

2226 **bi þat lace** 'measured against that belt, the brightly shining girdle'. Editors are divided as to whether the lace referred to is a counterpart of the thong lapped around the haft of the Green Knight's axe when he appeared at Camelot (*cf.* 217–20; TGD, Goll., And.) or an allusion to the green girdle Gawain is wearing when he faces the second axe at the Green Chapel (Wal., Bur.), as if the sight of the giant blade makes him instinctively compare it with the talisman whose power to protect him must be passing through his mind—'It was no less gruesome because of the girdle that gleamed full bright' (Van. trans.).

2297 **þe byȝe hode** The adjective suggests that it is not the specialised literal sense of *hode*—'the hood worn by … knights of chivalric orders' (MED *hod* n., 2(b))—which is intended here, but the 'order' of knighthood which Arthur had conferred upon Gawain. *Cf.* Sil. 'degree'.

2317–19 Despite the terms of the compact, by which there can be no resistance to the return blow, Gawain wears the full campaign dress of a knight and has his shield slung on his shoulder in such a position that a practised jerk makes it slide down the arm into a defensive position.

2387 **Leteȝ me ouertake your wylle** may mean simply 'Let me win your good will', but the verb can have a more specific sense, 'to apprehend mentally, to comprehend, understand' (OED *overtake* v., 5), suggesting here 'Let me understand your will (as to the penance I should do)'. The idea of penance is inherent in Gawain's 'confession' to Bertilak (2379–86) and the latter's response (2390–4), with its explicit use of technical language (*confessed*, *penaunce*). *Cf.* Goll., Wal.

2445 **de Hautdesert** Bertilak's title has been interpreted as 'of the high hermitage' and as a reference to the confessional functions which he shares with the hermits of certain spiritualised Arthurian romances. But the interpretation rests upon a specialised meaning of *disert* ('hermitage') in Celtic languages, whereas *desert* ('deserted or solitary place') is a familiar element in French place names and here no doubt refers to the Green Knight's castle. *Cf.* TGD.

2446–66 This passage refers to elements of Arthurian tradition which would be familiar to readers of romance. Uther, King of Britain, having become infatuated with the Duke of Tintagel's wife, was enabled by the enchantments of the wizard Merlin to beget Arthur upon her illicitly. The duchess already had a daughter,

Morgan, who was consequently Arthur's half-sister and Gawain's aunt. Merlin having fallen in love with her, Morgan so fascinated him that he taught her all his magic arts, by which she gained her reputation as a 'goddess'. Grown aged and ugly through trafficking with evil powers, she made malicious use of her magic, persecuting the forces of chivalry, Arthur's court and, in particular, Guinevere, who had once exposed an amorous intrigue of hers. Bertilak attributes his challenging of the repute of the Round Table to her malice and the Green Knight's appearance to her magic arts in a long sentence which is broken off (2448) and resumed (2456) with a new structure. Lines 2447–8 have not, perhaps, been well understood: the first is usually taken to refer to Morgan's powers, the second to their derivation from Merlin, but without any direct grammatical connection (*cf.* And., Wal.). If, however, *craftes* is taken as 'skill in deceiving, trickery' (MED *craft* n., 2(b)), both lines can be read, without hiatus, as a reference to the methods by which she obtained her powers—and, possibly, as another example of the evil influence of women in the lives of great men, as cited by Gawain (2414–26).

2506 **bende** can be simply 'band, ribbon', but in heraldry it has a more technical sense: 'a broad diagonal band or stripe placed on a coat of arms, banner, shield, etc.' (MED n.[1], 4)—usually drawn from dexter chief to sinister base, as Gawain wears the girdle over his right shoulder and fastened at his left side (2485–7).

2515 As Bur. suggests, the manuscript *lordes and ladis* is probably a mistake for *lordes and ledes* (*cf.* 38) since ladies would not normally be included in the brotherhood of the Round Table and *burne* (2516) implies that the reference is to male members only.

2522–3 The poem ends, as it began, by connecting the world of Arthur with the legendary history of Brutus. *Brutus bokeȝ* could include both British chronicles and Arthurian romances.

Hony soit … The Garter motto has been written at the end of the poem, apparently to associate it with that order, perhaps in allusion to the Round Table's adoption of the green girdle as a badge of chivalric honour. But the Garter sash was not green and there is no evidence that the poet himself intended any reference to the order.